4,800

of Uncle Boogs's Favorite Sayings *and* Phrases

ISBN 978-1-7357643-0-6

Cover design copyright © 2020 by Dave Kempa
Cover design by Patrick Dorsey

Book design by Patrick Dorsey
Typeset in Caslon and Gill Sans MT

Manufactured in the United States of America

4,800

of Uncle Boogs's Favorite Sayings *and* Phrases

(Man, that guy could talk good.)

Dave Kempa

This tome is dedicated to my parents Warren and Mary Jo and to my wife Mary. Each has been influential in shaping my wonderful life.

Contents

Introduction

"I'm sorry to inform you that your Uncle Boogs died earlier this morning. He was the victim of an unfortunate incident involving his oxygen tent and an errant cigar ash. I'm sorry for your loss. How soon can you claim the body?" That was a nurse from the Almost Heaven nursing home and it was the saddest day of my life.

I loved spending time with my uncle Boogs (/boōgs/, rhymes with *books*)—out in a fishing boat, street fighting, cookin' funnel cakes. He could talk for hours. What he lacked in intellect, he made up with by using colorful and intriguing phrases and vernacular. He could present his feeble ideas in such an engaging way, that you really thought there was some substance behind them. How I wished I had Uncle Boog's effortless ability to turn a phrase.

So, here's what I did: One afternoon, I got my Big Chief pad of paper and one of those fat pencils and I wrote down all of Uncle Boog's clever phrases. Almost word for word. No doubt, as you read them, many won't make sense. I asked Uncle Boogs if I should make every phrase perfectly understandable. He said, "Don't waste your time." Sometimes I didn't really know what he meant, but hearing it in context, it made sense at the time.

I'd ask Uncle Boogs if he invented his colorful witticisms. "Goodness, no. I've surrounded myself with bright people, funny people. I've read some Mark Twain and watched my share of Johnny Carson. No, I can't take credit for creating the phrases, but I take credit for assembling them into my lexicon. Like Baseball cards, stamps and art. Those collectors didn't create the objects, they created the collection."

I'm here to share them with you. Perhaps like me, you, too, can incorporate some of his stylings into your mundane patter to get the girl of your dreams, earn that promotion, or even be elected president of Peru.

Incidentally, you'll notice that the book is presented in a convenient checklist format to help you keep track of your favorites. Keep the book handy on your nightstand, or review it before your next big sales pitch.

BE SURE TO USE THE CHECKBOXES TO IDENTIFY YOUR FAVORITES FOR FUTURE STUDY!

I. Character (Or Names to Call People)

"I was going to sue for defamation of character, but then I realized I have no character."

Sure, Uncle Boogs was a character. I think he had his share of book learning. But he lived alone. Perhaps he was lonely. Now I'm not saying he had uncontrolled verbosity, but he could talk for hours. Trying to classify all of his phrases was tricky. In this chapter I've included words and phrases that can be used to describe personality, temperament, and physical traits. Some of these phrases become remarkably handy when you want to engage in some old-school name calling. Interestingly, most are derogatory.

☐ Feckless twit
☐ A tangled-headed old fool
☐ Tightwad
☐ He has a cracked memory chip.
☐ A sullen teenager
☐ Little, mean, and smirking
☐ George couldn't operate a Bic lighter.
☐ She's got a hairnet job at the diner.
☐ You have Cream of Wheat for brains.
☐ Ragu was his blood type.
☐ He was a bad winner, and an even worse loser.
☐ He goes to the Waffle House and orders pancakes.
☐ Untroubled by questions of ethics

HAVE YOU EVER BEEN CALLED UPON TO WRITE A LETTER OF RECOMMENDATION OR COMPLETE A PERFORMANCE APPRAISAL AND GRAPPLE FOR JUST THE RIGHT WORDS? USE THESE CHECKBOXES TO EARMARK PHRASES TO GIVE YOUR WRITING THE ACCURACY IT DESERVES.

☐ Forgot to pay his brain bill
☐ Swivel-eyed
☐ A mouth breather
☐ Outstandingly offensive
☐ A few beers short of a six pack
☐ Two-fold personality
☐ Infernal jackass
☐ He's killed people with his thumbs.
☐ My nickname used to be "Polyester Pants."
☐ Except for the beard, you remind me of my grandmother.
☐ I can see around corners.
☐ She had an alcohol-sodden body.
☐ Mr. Couldn't-Make-Matters-Worse just walked in.
☐ He got into the gene pool while the lifeguard wasn't watching.
☐ Somebody blew your pilot light out.
☐ They were hip in their own mind.
☐ He was all foam, no beer.
☐ Crazed sex poodle
☐ Well-scrubbed young man.
☐ The scourge of...
☐ Thin-lipped bow-legged child
☐ Macho shithead
☐ The professor couldn't zip his fly even if he had an instruction book.
☐ Stupidly handsome
☐ I think the butter slipped off your pancake.
☐ Mother figure
☐ A smoky lounge singer's voice
☐ You've got a 10-gallon hat but no cattle.
☐ Silver-tongued devil
☐ We don't chill the Merlot or let farm animals in the house at night.

☐ Bedraggled appearance

☐ You're the diet coke of evil, just one calorie isn't enough.

☐ He was considered to be a truth twister.

☐ Wearing the spats and high collars of the London banking tribe

☐ An intellect rivaled only by garden tools

☐ He became quarrelsome when touched by liquor.

☐ Sarah had a fondness for the jugged burgundies of California.

☐ Charlie doesn't know whether to scratch his ass or wind his watch.

☐ Squid brain

☐ Fell out of the stupid tree and hit every branch on the way down

☐ Cad

☐ Hot-blooded hawk

☐ A thick Christian smile

☐ The wardrobe of an assistant camp counselor at a low-budget bible college.

☐ Oscar was such a great man that even the undertaker was sad when he died.

☐ Blundering idiot

☐ You look like a before picture.

☐ Warhorse

☐ Old fool

☐ Epitome of virtue

☐ Gadfly

☐ Sense of decency and virtue

☐ He has used up all his life lines.

☐ You've got more guts than brains.

☐ Can't find his desk unless there's cheese on it.

☐ A haranguer

- [ ] A weak chin
- [ ] The scoutmaster was burly and pie-faced.
- [ ] He never dated a waitress from Perkins.
- [ ] Duane's a peanut-headed sample of nature's carelessness.
- [ ] Half-bubble off plumb
- [ ] There's snow on the roof but no fire in the furnace.
- [ ] Prune-face
- [ ] Cherubic-cheeked
- [ ] Takes him hour-and-a-half to watch *60 Minutes.*
- [ ] Charlie was a white shoe kind of guy.
- [ ] A brain the size of a cheerio
- [ ] Fartarounds
- [ ] His biscuit is not completely baked.
- [ ] He couldn't find his ass with a flashlight and a road map.
- [ ] He could talk a dog off a meat wagon,
- [ ] They're the kind of people you wouldn't want to invite to your party.
- [ ] A worthy adversary
- [ ] Lacks talents in all arts, master of no skills, jack of no trades
- [ ] Cry-baby
- [ ] CAVE people (Citizens Against Virtually Everything)
- [ ] Amiable dunce
- [ ] He's the kind of eater who butters his butter.
- [ ] I used to work for a guy who was often wrong, and never in doubt.
- [ ] Three anchovies short of a pizza
- [ ] Hapless
- [ ] She wore a bruised ego.
- [ ] Bloated persona
- [ ] Mental midget with the IQ of a fence post
- [ ] Your mind is full of sawdust.
- [ ] If brains were taxed, he'd get a rebate.

- ☐ Jolly good fellow
- ☐ Chump
- ☐ You sober son of a gun you
- ☐ A Philistine
- ☐ Stinking of moth balls
- ☐ I'd characterize Robin as an elderly gentleman, versus an old codger.
- ☐ You've been a raspberry seed in my wisdom tooth.
- ☐ Shriveled wine sack
- ☐ Quarrelsome when touched by liquor
- ☐ A pock-marked faced 30-year-old
- ☐ Meaty palms
- ☐ Dimwitted hatred
- ☐ Norah was a legion in her own mind.
- ☐ If you stand close enough to him you can hear the ocean.
- ☐ A few clowns short of a circus
- ☐ He had a neck wider than his head.
- ☐ Blithe-hearted
- ☐ As a baby, I was left on the Tilt-A-Whirl a bit too long.
- ☐ The city's most notorious grump
- ☐ When he broke his leg, gravy poured out.
- ☐ Keith is a backstabbing backstabber.
- ☐ Pine tree-hugging, croissant-eating…
- ☐ A white tasseled loafer
- ☐ Wise guy
- ☐ He spent his entire career breaking the spirit of colleagues.
- ☐ He was awash in snot and tears.
- ☐ A lunatic's grin
- ☐ She had a meaty neck.
- ☐ Booby hatched
- ☐ Just dumb enough to be fearless and just bright enough to be dangerous.

- ☐ Odd duck
- ☐ He had a heart the size of a baby's head.
- ☐ Chet doesn't know if it's Tuesday or September.
- ☐ She was Mary, Mohamad, and Vishnu.
- ☐ Heavy in the bottom
- ☐ Sucker
- ☐ A man of honor and discretion who can be trusted.
- ☐ Stooge
- ☐ Gordon's antenna doesn't pick up all the channels.
- ☐ A room-temperature IQ
- ☐ Ray could not muster a teaspoon of optimism.
- ☐ You squashed cabbage leaf!
- ☐ Bilingual illiterate (can't read in two languages)
- ☐ His receiver is off the hook
- ☐ Corn-headed children
- ☐ Bill's think tank needs a new float valve.
- ☐ She had showgirl gams.
- ☐ Got a full six-pack, but lacks the plastic thingy to hold them together.
- ☐ Proverbial rear end
- ☐ Underconfident
- ☐ She had bedroom eyes and dining room lips.
- ☐ You seem to be one of those guys who PRETENDS to like jazz.
- ☐ Babe magnet
- ☐ Dumb cluck
- ☐ Rubenesque
- ☐ Jock-snappers
- ☐ So cool, he has a candy bowl of condoms on his night stand.
- ☐ A few tacos short of a platter
- ☐ Cheese-eating surrender monkeys
- ☐ Small-minded xenophobe

- [ ] She was beyond the pale of respectability.
- [ ] Trailer park trash
- [ ] Teenage dirt bag
- [ ] Joyless adults
- [ ] He is a minor head injury away from eating his own doo doo.
- [ ] He's one tough stone to chip
- [ ] The big magilla
- [ ] A floundering cod
- [ ] Douchebags, a bunch of douchebags…
- [ ] Flim-flam man
- [ ] He may look like an idiot and talk like an idiot, but don't let that fool you. He really is an idiot.
- [ ] Leon's not the sharpest knife in the drawer.
- [ ] A capsized ego
- [ ] A blob-o-protoplasm…a newborn
- [ ] I'm one of those crusty old bastards walking, farting, and wandering around in my underwear.
- [ ] She had a hunger for change.
- [ ] You know you're ugly when a nymphomaniac likes you as a friend.
- [ ] In the pinball game of life, Bruno's flippers are a little further apart than most.
- [ ] Fiona was a woman with dough-colored skin.
- [ ] Congenitally adverse
- [ ] Two arrows short of a quiver
- [ ] She's the kind of girl you'd meet in a sushi bar last call.
- [ ] This lovely creature
- [ ] A Bambi-eyed sophomore
- [ ] A pain in the pants
- [ ] Dolt
- [ ] Herb has a bias toward action.
- [ ] He's dead but won't lie down.

☐ His mind is like a piñata—when it cracks open, a lot of surprises come out.

☐ Going to hell on a scholarship

☐ She was a hardened woman who wore red lipstick, resorted to smoking Lucky's, and unnatural forms of sex.

☐ Victim of inertia

☐ The once-bombastic Senator

☐ Godless sodomites

☐ An inert sack of flatulent flesh on the couch

☐ A fawn-like girl

☐ Her fat face had a little smear of stale lipstick.

☐ Louis is a living brain donor

☐ Dunderhead

☐ The Apostle of Common Sense

☐ Analog man

☐ A run-of-the-mall kid

☐ Angular turnip

☐ One neuron short of a synapse

☐ His oil was leaking and the wheels were coming off.

☐ Dummkopf

☐ She could suck-start a Harley.

☐ Bobby had the frame of a sports walker.

☐ Technically illiterate

☐ Extremely normal

☐ Bare-knuckled meanness

☐ He's so smart he knows the identity of the Unknown Soldier.

☐ The able Mr. So-and-so

☐ Some people drink from the fountain of knowledge; Bonnie, she just gargled.

☐ I don't think his seatback tray is in the upright position.

☐ Hopelessly pubescent

☐ Layabouts

- [ ] You are as observant as you are beautiful.
- [ ] Mr. Greaseball
- [ ] Hardened infidels
- [ ] Girls of the trailer park
- [ ] Heel
- [ ] Flea-bitten
- [ ] You're playing hockey with a warped puck.
- [ ] An anchor without a ship
- [ ] Be counted among men like Albert Einstein, Albert Schweitzer, Mark Twain, Carl Sandburg, Bing Crosby, Norman Rockwell, and (your company CEO)
- [ ] She was economical with the truth.
- [ ] A few sandwiches short of a picnic
- [ ] Well-intentioned but misguided
- [ ] Old codger
- [ ] The prettiest girl at the dance
- [ ] Strange duck
- [ ] Clinically insane
- [x] Your head looks like a piece of urban folk-art.
- [ ] Cold-blooded
- [ ] He's so dense that light bends around him.
- [ ] Vulcan mindset
- [x] Fell out of the ugly tree and hit every branch on the way down
- [ ] You shabby napkin
- [ ] Rainforest man
- [ ] He is a just man who fears the Lord and shuns evil.
- [ ] He's orbiting in space without a rudder and no solid fuel booster to get on course.
- [ ] He put real horse power in the term motor mouth.
- [ ] Flight risk
- [ ] Nancy boy
- [ ] He's worse than the crabs.

- ☐ A man of letters
- ☐ He's a plane that crashes every day.
- ☐ My little sponge cake
- ☐ Marty was a human platitude.
- ☐ A kind of guy who doesn't dance in the endzone.
- ☐ Cheapskate
- ☐ You've got more going for you than flapping nostrils.
- ☐ Large Marge
- ☐ A tractor trailer of a man
- ☐ Indifferent to vice
- ☐ A drug-soaked mentality
- ☐ Incurable idiot
- ☐ Sick puppy
- ☐ A real square egg
- ☐ A few peas short of a casserole
- ☐ The wheel's spinning but the hamster's dead.
- ☐ Capacity for laziness
- ☐ Julie reminds me of Lulu from *Hee Haw.*
- ☐ Looks like you enter a lot of pie eating contests.
- ☐ Can't hit a note with a shotgun
- ☐ Such a bunch of stupes
- ☐ He's the kind of guy who could follow you in a revolving door and come out ahead of you.
- ☐ You're full of sap.
- ☐ Checked his dipstick and he was a quart low
- ☐ The Beloved Brethren
- ☐ Ignoramus
- ☐ Bonehead
- ☐ Lout
- ☐ He is a walking flat-line.
- ☐ Earl's a reasoning machine. (in reference to a person)
- ☐ Marty didn't realize he was standing on his own air hose.
- ☐ Anaconda, my locker room nickname

- ☐ You're fruit
- ☐ Bill passed the smell test
- ☐ Luddites
- ☐ A man favored by God
- ☐ He was one of those guys who chewed wooden matches and wore a ball cap with sweat stains resembling tree rings.
- ☐ Ill-tempered
- ☐ You look like you just shot somebody.
- ☐ Earl couldn't pour piss out of a boot if the directions were printed on the heel.
- ☐ She's a Monet—looks good at a distance, but not up close.
- ☐ A coughing dissident
- ☐ Roy had the survival instincts of a stray dog.
- ☐ The substitute teacher was the kind of gal who wore all her clothing a half size too tight, thus making her pleasing contours…well-displayed.
- ☐ Dog face.
- ☐ One Froot Loop short of a full bowl
- ☐ A big galoot
- ☐ A lionized hero
- ☐ The workers at Culver's are always well-scrubbed.
- ☐ He lives under a rock
- ☐ So-and-so is not well screwed in.
- ☐ Loafing, good-natured no-account
- ☐ Your handwriting looks like your medications need to be adjusted.
- ☐ Hereditary imbecility
- ☐ A loud and arrogant pant load
- ☐ My kindergarten teacher reminded me of a character in a Russian novel.
- ☐ Imbecile
- ☐ Human driftwood
- ☐ Seadog-faced

- ☐ Shameless hussies
- ☐ Excuse me Donald, you sub-literate, gum-bleeding booger-eater...
- ☐ The substitute teacher was pale but jubilant.
- ☐ Sufficient moral fiber
- ☐ Neo-pagan
- ☐ Etta's the kind of gal who douses a fire with gasoline.
- ☐ Handicap between the ears
- ☐ Fertile imagination
- ☐ Self-effacing
- ☐ You've got splinters in the windmill of your mind.
- ☐ A twenty-five-year-old yoga instructor with low self-esteem
- ☐ One taco short of a combination plate
- ☐ A few fries short of a Happy Meal
- ☐ Missing a few buttons on his remote-control
- ☐ A sack-like chin
- ☐ Beefcake
- ☐ He was a Pharisee's Pharisee
- ☐ Dirt balls
- ☐ Tripehound
- ☐ He packed four years of college into five.
- ☐ You have so much culture they could name a yogurt after you.
- ☐ VICTIM...tattooed on his forehead
- ☐ Jim's favorite actor is Barney Rubble.
- ☐ Nutcase
- ☐ Didn't know the difference between Hamas and hummus
- ☐ You couldn't get a swear word out of Chris even if you squeezed him with a pair of pliers.
- ☐ Roger had a loose grasp on reality.
- ☐ Like everybody else, during day one of rehab, Sarah was combative and truculent.

☐ His high school photo was an aerial photo.
☐ Butterfingers
☐ He's been sober for 480 days, not all in a row.
☐ Nutjob
☐ I think Gerard's chimney's clogged.
☐ A quivering mass of contradictions
☐ The universal wit of cretins, young and old
☐ My old girlfriend was a large, radioactive bucket of stress.
☐ Full of vim and vigor
☐ A grizzled man
☐ Bill's a model prisoner
☐ Roustabouts
☐ A walking flat line
☐ Dismal failure
☐ She Who Must Be Obeyed
☐ Reeks of integrity
☐ He spent his youth among strumpets and petty thieves.
☐ Asshat
☐ Joan's head is in dark places
☐ A person not wanting in shrewdness and common sense
☐ An unprincipled man
☐ Paul demonstrated the loyalty of Gunga Din.
☐ Little shaver
☐ Harry's belt doesn't go through all the loops.
☐ Foster Brooks behavior, and not in a funny way
☐ Pig-headed
☐ A high-pitched sandpaper voice
☐ Marty was famous for his wise counsel.
☐ A pancake without syrup
☐ A placid and dignified countenance
☐ Don was a silver-tongued imbecile.
☐ He wouldn't say shit if he had a mouth full of it.
☐ You drive like Starsky AND Hutch.

- ☐ You look like you're wearing colostomy pants.
- ☐ Jerry's elevator doesn't go anywhere near the top floor.
- ☐ Fallen from grace
- ☐ Don't be that guy in college who hand-paints bird feeders and sells them at the weekend craft fair wearing a jester cap and performing a juggling routine.
- ☐ A pain in the ear
- ☐ Her cooking could make the lame walk.
- ☐ Rubes
- ☐ A man too busy to flush toilets
- ☐ Percy couldn't get laid in a woman's prison.
- ☐ Living death
- ☐ Small potato aristocrat
- ☐ Marginal people
- ☐ A suffering servant
- ☐ Outstandingly offensive
- ☐ His skylight leaks a little
- ☐ Happy-go-lucky
- ☐ Pleated chin
- ☐ A chronically carping spouse
- ☐ He's the kind of guy who eats on both sides of the buffet.
- ☐ No grain in his silo
- ☐ Basket case
- ☐ Couldn't hit water if he fell out of a boat
- ☐ You were only a splinter as I slid down the banister of life.
- ☐ You remind me of one of those people who drink tea from an oversized mug with two hands, wearing an oversized sweater.
- ☐ He's a plane that crashes every day.
- ☐ Chuckleheads
- ☐ Plagued with verbal diarrhea
- ☐ Equal opportunity offender
- ☐ Street urchins

- ☐ Dubious and questionable character
- ☐ Fruit cake
- ☐ He was a shape-shifting individual.
- ☐ Hapless scallywag
- ☐ Toad-eyed
- ☐ His Nimbleness
- ☐ Sweet patootie
- ☐ There are only two people in the world with your blood type, Ernest and Julio Gallo.
- ☐ You sound like one of those screwballs who live on millionaire hill.
- ☐ Serial liar
- ☐ He showed signs of a poisoned mind.
- ☐ Lives in a vacuum
- ☐ Cabbage head
- ☐ Dwight couldn't make it with $20 in a two-bit whore house.
- ☐ She dresses like a Goodwill mannequin.
- ☐ Does he have his bait in the water?
- ☐ A slab of a man
- ☐ Birkenstock people
- ☐ Doesn't have all his cornflakes in one box
- ☐ A sad sack
- ☐ A pack of flat heads
- ☐ Cactus head
- ☐ Self-loathing
- ☐ Good egg
- ☐ She wore her brand-new jean skort with pride.
- ☐ That clown
- ☐ An affinity for the wrong guess
- ☐ So-and-so is not tightly wrapped.
- ☐ A drug-soaked life

- ☐ You look like the kind of guy who likes to get in a hot tub and watch your swim trunks inflate.
- ☐ Affable sage
- ☐ Infested with fleas
- ☐ Baggy-suited bastard
- ☐ A photographic memory, but the lens cover is glued on
- ☐ Movie star handsome, with a Peposdent smile
- ☐ A man possessed
- ☐ Fresh-faced
- ☐ A tractor trailer of a man
- ☐ Valedictorian at summer school
- ☐ The folds on the back of his neck reminds one of a pack of hot dogs.
- ☐ The grumpy dog
- ☐ He is not a profile in courage
- ☐ You make coffee nervous
- ☐ Morally ambiguous
- ☐ Elevator doesn't go all the way to the top floor
- ☐ Mark had spaghetti for brains.
- ☐ Her sewing machine out of thread.
- ☐ An honest wag
- ☐ Sick puppy
- ☐ Little rebel
- ☐ Pencil necked
- ☐ Philanderer
- ☐ A bag of knowledge
- ☐ Pompous pontificator
- ☐ Jill's moral dipstick is two drops short of dry.
- ☐ Latte-sipping liberals
- ☐ A slothful wench
- ☐ Square-headed girlfriend
- ☐ Industrial strength stupid
- ☐ They were drunk on their own testosterone.

- ☐ The gates are down, the lights are flashing, but the train isn't coming.
- ☐ Adel had a cherubic but naughty looking face.
- ☐ Voted best Christian woman in America
- ☐ Maria was the other half of my heartbeat.
- ☐ He had a rubber face
- ☐ Little monsters
- ☐ A jaded, thick-skinned group of thrill seekers
- ☐ Jolly people
- ☐ Patrician figure
- ☐ Judy is that kind of girl that would wear a leotard under her dress.
- ☐ The humility gene was not passed along to that individual.
- ☐ Half-breed
- ☐ Beneath my cold exterior, once you break the ice, you find cold water.
- ☐ Plain, plump, and dowdy with a fierce temper and a foul mouth.
- ☐ Amy was one of those non-arousing red heads.
- ☐ Corrosive hostility
- ☐ A marinated brain
- ☐ Lady with a baffled look
- ☐ Irascible reprobate
- ☐ Direly pessimistic
- ☐ A ragged street urchin
- ☐ The Merchant of Venom
- ☐ There's no filter on this brain
- ☐ Raisin-skinned face
- ☐ Justin is not the coldest drink in the refrigerator.
- ☐ The composure of a knife thrower's assistant
- ☐ Louse
- ☐ A bastion of knowledge

- ☐ Leggy cocktail waitress among beefy tourists
- ☐ Jean had no more brains that a tree stump.
- ☐ Crazier than seven daredevil iron workers hopped up on Jack Daniels
- ☐ You slumped-shouldered sack of nuts!
- ☐ Panty sniffer
- ☐ Under the influence of sodium pentothal
- ☐ Hardscrabbled
- ☐ He was a messiah's messiah.
- ☐ He was all pants and no trousers.
- ☐ A walking nimbus cloud
- ☐ The nicest thing to say about her is that all her tattoos were spelled correctly.
- ☐ You little piss-soaked bastard
- ☐ You are the ink in my pen
- ☐ Elephantine people
- ☐ He was the best hated man in town.
- ☐ He thinks he was born in Bethlehem.
- ☐ Hapless scallywag
- ☐ Blinking idiot
- ☐ Bowmar Brain
- ☐ Poor screw
- ☐ Patty was a five-alarm fire of talent and charisma.
- ☐ You can see Kim's charisma from space.
- ☐ A flannel shirt-wearing goober
- ☐ Fairytale figures
- ☐ She could sing the phone book and make it sound great.
- ☐ Hideous-looking
- ☐ Squig-faced bird stuffer
- ☐ A sadly crouching cross-eyed man with a beak of a nose and a face that danced with nervous tics
- ☐ He's the kind of guy who goes right to the edge and folds it neatly.

- [ ] Otis's a real toothache of a man.
- [ ] She was a feckless gossip; careless, sluttish, lazy, and unfaithful.
- [ ] Fidelity-ridden life
- [ ] Fish lips
- [ ] A ginger-hair, snub-nose man in dungarees.
- [ ] You look like death on toast.
- [ ] Victim mindset
- [ ] He claims he took the red pill, but I think he needs a suppository.
- [ ] Husky
- [ ] Dora had a heart as soft as a mouse's underbelly but could be as hard as steel.
- [ ] Butterfingers
- [ ] Couldn't get a standing ovation if the seats were on fire
- [ ] I think a few of your lug nuts are starting to loosen.
- [ ] Walking around like he had a load in his pants.
- [ ] The tusks of nose hair gave him character.
- [ ] Maxwell was such a particular carpenter that he would put a level on his level.
- [ ] You are the horseradish in my Bloody Mary.
- [ ] The mental capacity of a soap dish
- [ ] Didn't know the difference between a boll weevil and a cotton ball

2. Analogies

Analogy (/əˈnaləjē/): a comparison between two things, typically for the purpose of explanation or clarification.

Admittedly, what follows are not all analogies. However most contain words like *that, as, like,* and *than.*

- ☐ Warts the size of new potatoes
- ☐ Taking a hamster to the vet is like having a disposable lighter repaired.
- ☐ More dangerous than a fatalistic Zen monk
- ☐ His black hair was so thick and perfectly groomed that it looked like something from a furrier shelf.
- ☐ Graveyard Dead
- ☐ Cars so safe that the crash dummies die of old age
- ☐ It was so hot that, if you threw a frozen hamburger up, when it came down it was cooked. If you threw it up too far, it came down burned.
- ☐ Cruise ships so big they have bad neighborhoods
- ☐ You look like death on a biscuit.
- ☐ Stiffer than a sun-dried frog on a Texas highway
- ☐ Sweating like a Wyoming hooker on cowboy payday
- ☐ Screaming like a stray cat caught in a screen door
- ☐ Wearing enough makeup to scare a hooker
- ☐ My bones are shaking like dice on a Las Vegas craps table.

- [ ] I feel like the world's a tuxedo and I'm a pair of brown shoes.
- [ ] I slept like a dead man.
- [ ] When I shook his hand, it was like he was wearing an oven mitt.
- [ ] Used to cry like babies
- [ ] Dancing like a washing machine
- [ ] Meat cooked so rare that it still has a heartbeat

If your vocabulartory is limited to words like fake, not good, boring, stupid and great, you need some help.

Check off a few of these gems to try this week!

- [ ] Pleased as punch
- [ ] As hard a Chinese math
- [ ] Clinging to her like a suckling piglet to its mother
- [ ] As deaf as a post
- [ ] He's from so deep in the country he's got corn growing in his shoes.
- [ ] That's like calling King Kong a monkey.
- [ ] I haven't tasted anything this bad since I had to suck start my chainsaw.
- [ ] As easy as rolling off a log
- [ ] Like taking vitamins with soda
- [ ] Like trying to kill a snake
- [ ] Breath so bad it could peel wall paper
- [ ] As sad as a coven of overweight Wiccans sitting around eating chocolate cake
- [ ] That rumor spread like the norovirus through a Pilates class.
- [ ] Tiny moles were scattered across her face like buckshot.
- [ ] He was acting like a bully on the playground.
- [ ] As quiet and unassuming as Amish farmers
- [ ] Clearer than a momma's bell

☐ Like trying to pick up a turd by the clean end

☐ Like being in a lion's den with pork chop breeches

☐ Bank rolls as big as ham sandwiches

☐ When I was a kid, we were so poor that I had to play baseball with an oven mitt.

☐ As rare as a woman with three nostrils

☐ Greatest thing since canned dog food

☐ The strength of nine devils

☐ He was so boring that someone drew a chalk outline around his body.

☐ Skin so dry it was a fire hazard

☐ As dead as a fried oyster

☐ I'm like the daffodil that spreads fragrance on the heel of that which crushes it.

☐ The child who cries in vain is like the humming bird who uses Hi-C for motor oil.

☐ Sing like Al Jolson

☐ Shit so hard I think I sprained my asshole

☐ The guys had tears running down their faces like three suddenly repentant Nazis boys who were just caught tearing hymnal pockets off the back of pews.

☐ Feeling like a minnow in a dipnet

☐ He's got more hair in his ears than on his head.

☐ Clean as mustard

☐ Staggered around like an elephant hit with a tranquilizer dart

☐ I feel like an oyster feeding off the effluent flowing from the sewer of right-wing dishonesty.

☐ The fire station bunkroom smelled of the tart belch of low octane gasoline.

☐ Like the feeling you get when you lock your keys in the car

☐ Worse than Hitler

☐ So old that it was built when Jesus was in third grade

- [ ] News of the crime spread like gophers in a golf course.
- [ ] We were so poor, my dad hung Jiffy Pop over my bed as a smoke detector. Now every time I walk past a popcorn machine I stop, drop, and roll.
- [ ] He was so big, after he was diagnosed with flesh eating disease, he was given fourteen years to live.
- [ ] As popular as a nark at a bike's rally
- [ ] The adolescent teenage couple were exchanging genetic information like computer hackers exchange software.
- [ ] Wound tighter than a nine-day clock
- [ ] Like doing a heroin deal with Mr. Rogers
- [ ] Smoother that a fresh jar of Skippy
- [ ] As rare as hen's teeth
- [ ] More loop holes than a spiral notebook
- [ ] Melted like butter on a hot waffle
- [ ] Hotter than a hooker on nickel night
- [ ] Scabs the size of pepperonis
- [ ] Her voice was so bad that during the Star Spangled Banner, an usher asked her to stop.
- [ ] Busier than a one-legged bobcat trying to cover his crap on a frozen pond
- [ ] My abs, over the years, have become a pale downward-leaning sack of fat, not unlike a drooping Salvador Dali clockface.
- [ ] Like rearranging the deck chairs on the *Titanic*
- [ ] The girls hung around him like teeny boppers hang around Wolfman Jack at the malt shop.
- [ ] In Las Vegas I dropped more money than pants at the Kennedy compound.
- [ ] As thrilling as Wally Cox's underwear
- [ ] We go together like Chinese food and chocolate pudding.
- [ ] Like trying to keep frogs in a wheelbarrow
- [ ] That came apart like an Alka Seltzer under Niagara Falls.
- [ ] We rolled that Camaro like a cowboy cigarette.

- [ ] As dead as a stuffed mongoose
- [ ] Hot sauce so powerful that tankers carrying it had to space themselves by 500 feet, travel at night, and detour around major population centers
- [ ] Played me like a two-bit piccolo
- [ ] A riot so big that the police ran out of handcuffs
- [ ] Growing up, I was so poor the rainbows were in black and white.
- [ ] He was so crooked, when he died, they had to screw him in the ground.
- [ ] So windy that when a chicken turned her back to the wind, she laid the same egg six times
- [ ] Smarter than a Roomba
- [ ] So-and-so fears bees like the devil fears holy water.
- [ ] He is so old, every picture of him is in sepia tone, with a whale oil lamp, as he churns butter
- [ ] Chili so hot that it will blow your hat into the creek
- [ ] The bunks in the old fishing trawler were kippered by the grime and sweat of use by crusty fishermen.
- [ ] More fun than Tetris and Solitaire
- [ ] Her body was as cold as yesterday's toast
- [ ] Fought like a Comanche
- [ ] Like playing a finely tuned piano
- [ ] Legs so withered their profile resembled hockey sticks
- [ ] So quiet you could hear a pin drop in a jar of marshmallow sauce
- [ ] As happy as a dead pig in the sun
- [ ] We go together like cocaine and waffles.
- [ ] It's better than a sharp stick in the eye.
- [ ] Drop you like a cup of cold poison
- [ ] Cigars so strong that they kill at 30 feet
- [ ] As rough as a cob
- [ ] Politicians hand out lies like Catholics hand out guilt.
- [ ] Coffee cups the size of waste paper baskets

- He folded like a lawn chair.
- It was so cold, lawyers were walking down the street with their hands in their OWN pockets.
- As sure as a barn door has splinters
- Like chewing on a chunk of meat the size of a coin purse
- More painful than a Brazilian wax job
- You look like you've been scared by a burglar.
- She had a personality like seltzer water.
- Wet the bed so much, the mattress looks like an old coffee filter
- Like the dog chained up outside Starbucks
- Portions so small that you had to belch to know what it tasted like
- Her wrinkled face reminded me of a shucked pecan.
- I opened the email with as much fear and trepidation as opening a box of rattlesnakes.
- Meaner than a rooster
- You've got more balls than a Chinese ping-pong tournament.
- This is what I look like after treating myself like a trash can for fifty years.
- I'll tell you how humid it is…It's stickier than a Vietnamese woman working in a peanut brittle factory.
- The banking industry is in such bad shape that the Feds are offering the banks toasters and socket sets.
- Like a hand grenade thrown into the Sunday school picnic
- That plaid skirt looks like Kansas from the air.
- Like burning your money to keep warm
- As snug as a candle in a candle mold
- She wore a diamond the size of Mickey Rooney.
- Tighter than two thumbs in an asshole
- Madder that a one-legged waitress at IHOP
- Like that look of Thomas Jefferson when they told him they were going to free the slaves

☐ As simple as making a round wheel, but nobody thought of it

☐ The guys who just came into the bar look like two goofs from East Bumblefuck.

☐ You look like a tramp who would steal a chicken from someone's back yard.

☐ It was so sad, we were drying our eyes on each other's sleeves.

☐ His pickup truck was so big that I expected to see other trucks suckling on it.

☐ The same look that the priest in *The Exorcist* had when Linda Blair spit pea soup in his face

☐ More enthusiasm than a QVC salesperson after a six-pack of Red Bull

☐ As dead as vaudeville

☐ Easier to grow than a toenail

☐ The song was so sweet you could get a cavity just by listening to it.

☐ She looks mean enough to chew nails.

☐ A crust as hard as a ten-day old loaf of bread

☐ He can cut through bullshit like ammonia on the back of a greasy stove.

☐ Greed is like warm beer—it tastes like lizard piss.

☐ Sweating like a meth head

☐ She had a body that could make a bishop kick out a stained-glass window.

☐ As rich as Scrooge McDuck

☐ So stupid, she didn't even know how to breathe

☐ Shivering like I was operating a jackhammer

☐ You look like you were embalmed and it wore off.

☐ Smelling like a fraternity house carpet

☐ She was as pretty as a prayer book.

☐ The reporters gathered like maggots on a rotting corpse.

☐ I feel like a motherless child.

- ☐ My mouth was so dry I couldn't lick a stamp.
- ☐ You're trying to make water run uphill.
- ☐ I'm going to roll you like wholesale carpet.
- ☐ That suit is old enough to have kids in college.
- ☐ Living life like Don King: Spending money on women and wine and squandering all the rest
- ☐ Bill was so serious, you'd have thought he was making a hostage tape.
- ☐ I got stomped like a nark at a biker rally.
- ☐ She walked down more aisles than a vendor at a Dodger's game.
- ☐ She had the voice of a nuclear reactor wrapped in the body of an angel.
- ☐ Harder than hallelujah
- ☐ Like being the biggest turd in a urinal
- ☐ Swim meets that lasted longer than the Spanish-American War
- ☐ As solid as oak
- ☐ Coffee more potent than drain cleaner
- ☐ More chins than a Chinese phone book
- ☐ That babe is hotter than Atlanta asphalt.
- ☐ I like to eat at diners where there's biscuits, grits, and gravy, and the waitress calls you "baby."
- ☐ Sweating so bad I thought I had malaria
- ☐ So dark, you couldn't see your face in front of your hand
- ☐ Skittering around like a cockroach on a hot skillet
- ☐ Mad as cheese
- ☐ As colorless as the inside of a gopher's hole
- ☐ A city so wholesome that it ran out Donny Marie Osmond
- ☐ It was so cold, men were hugging after sex.
- ☐ As solid as Illinois livestock
- ☐ As right as rain
- ☐ Milk so old that it had a picture of the Lindbergh baby on it

- ☐ I'm so hungry my stomach thinks my throat has been slit.
- ☐ Like a hand grenade, it requires constant pressure to keep it from exploding.
- ☐ As leery of outsiders as the Vatican
- ☐ More scalp than hair
- ☐ Simple as a pimple
- ☐ Those girls were so rough, they used sandpaper as toilet paper.
- ☐ Ears the size of plates
- ☐ She had a body that could melt a cheese sandwich from across the room and breasts that seemed to say "Hey, look at these."
- ☐ A fist the size of a Sunday roast
- ☐ His grip was like shaking hands with a bag of circus peanuts.
- ☐ The winner of the hairy chest contest looked like he was wearing a sweater.
- ☐ The last time this many liberals were beaten so bad, they were being clubbed by the Chicago police.
- ☐ Whiter than the underbelly of a catfish
- ☐ As offensive as phlegm-covered saliva
- ☐ Like trying to teach a dog a card trick
- ☐ As smart as bait
- ☐ As spontaneous as the time of day
- ☐ She's as phony as fake nails.
- ☐ The house was so poorly built that it had papier-mâché steps.
- ☐ Quicker than two shakes of a lamb's tail
- ☐ This office is starting to look a lot like a hand basket.
- ☐ His ass was as firm as canned hams.
- ☐ As dated as a peacenik's ponytail
- ☐ Smells like someone deep fried doo doo in here.
- ☐ That dame sports more ice (diamonds) than the Arctic Circle.

- ☐ I can hold my breath like a manatee.
- ☐ It was like a hobbit walked into a room of tango dancers.
- ☐ Like a German complaining that he can't find a good bagel in Berlin anymore
- ☐ As different as chalk and cheese
- ☐ The nerve of a wounded tiger
- ☐ You're so late I thought you were coming by dog sled.
- ☐ He was so big that his shadow weighed forty-two pounds.
- ☐ Tighter than a lid on a pickle jar
- ☐ Jeans as tight as sunburn
- ☐ Darker than the inside of a cow
- ☐ As labor intensive as having a baby
- ☐ Like a lamp post for a drunk—support and not illumination
- ☐ They fought like Luke Skywalker and Darth Vader.
- ☐ Like a midget at a urinal, I was going to have to stay on my toes.
- ☐ I need that like Custer needed more Indians.
- ☐ I feel like the offender in a mouthwash commercial.
- ☐ He's such a smooth talker that he can make a pregnant woman think she's a virgin.
- ☐ As dead as a smoked herring
- ☐ Treated like a box of old hammers
- ☐ Eating out of your palms like they're full of cheese
- ☐ Drunker than Cooter Jones
- ☐ The wind blew so hard that when it stopped, the chickens fell over.
- ☐ Wasn't worth more than a mouth full of ashes
- ☐ Grandma was so big that it took three days to give her a hug.
- ☐ More laid back than the Dalai Lama
- ☐ Air so humid it was like breathing cream of mushroom soup
- ☐ As happy as a bat in a banana tree

- ☐ That car can't outrun a fat man.
- ☐ Like meeting Bugs Bunny in person
- ☐ The pitcher hit the batter's helmet so hard, it spun around fast enough that his eyebrows got burned off.
- ☐ So thirsty, I feel like I just sucked bone marrow from King Tut
- ☐ Diarrhea so bad it sounded like a hail storm on a farm pond
- ☐ Like drinking water from a fire hose
- ☐ As big as a silo
- ☐ More of a chance than me giving birth to a penguin than...
- ☐ Camouflaged hunters think that animals can't see them. That's like a moose coming into your family room with a picture of a coffee table on its back.
- ☐ Spoiled like a rotten oyster
- ☐ That air conditioner eats up current like a boll weevil on cotton.
- ☐ Chicken fingers so old that they had arthritis
- ☐ He looked like a deer caught in headlights.
- ☐ Tougher than beef jerky
- ☐ As reliable as a wood stove
- ☐ That was so long ago the earth's crust was still warm.
- ☐ She had a voice so husky it could pull a dog sled.
- ☐ Like putting a sword through my heart
- ☐ Meaner than a dog shitting tacks
- ☐ Like turning the Queen Mary around
- ☐ Legs so spindly it looks like she growed 'em last week
- ☐ As close as lips and teeth
- ☐ As dead as an iced catfish
- ☐ Tougher than a two-dollar steak
- ☐ The room was sweat-your-pants hot.
- ☐ Snored so loud that it knocked the alarm clock off the nightstand

- ☐ Eat like a farm hand
- ☐ Curled up like a jumbo shrimp
- ☐ Hotter than a scalded dog
- ☐ He drives like he's out of cigarettes.
- ☐ Fingers the size of bratwursts
- ☐ They kicked butt like Patton at Gettysburg.
- ☐ His face looked like a Zagnut bar.
- ☐ Nothing moves faster that a scary rumor.
- ☐ As spry as a cricket
- ☐ Dryer than an August fart
- ☐ I'm going to flip you like a cheese omelet!
- ☐ Like trying to polish an old turd, it is only going to get so shiny.
- ☐ As common as lips on a rooster
- ☐ He was passing more gas than a Hummer.
- ☐ My heart is thumping like a cat in a clothes dryer.
- ☐ As right as a trade wind
- ☐ He had a chip on his shoulder the size of a Pontiac.
- ☐ I feel like I've been locked in the fun house for three days.
- ☐ Tougher than Marine boot camp
- ☐ Like a lush wandering through his alcohol wilderness.
- ☐ I feel excited like, like I have a girlfriend!
- ☐ My wife saw more labor than Jimmy Hoffa.
- ☐ As plain as white bread
- ☐ He smelled so bad that she set off smoke detectors.
- ☐ Her prom date was so slimy that you'd think he would leave a grease trail behind him.
- ☐ The obstetrician used forceps on the baby's skull like it was a walnut.
- ☐ It was so cold, I saw two dogs trying to jump start a rabbit.
- ☐ As serious as toe fungus
- ☐ So old, he carries a pony express card

- ☐ Like stink on Iran
- ☐ As smug as a fat house cat
- ☐ This place looks like the inside of a goat's stomach.
- ☐ As common as shoes
- ☐ The bar was so smoky, you could cure hams in there.
- ☐ It was so cold, people were pouring McDonald's coffee on themselves and not suing.
- ☐ Worse than useless
- ☐ As useless as a one-legged man at an ass kicking session
- ☐ The Chernobyl of St Louis
- ☐ As dead as AM radio
- ☐ That's like buying teeth in the mail.
- ☐ Tougher than boiled owl
- ☐ Such a fast eater, she had racing stripes on her fork
- ☐ The house smelled of man sweat, spaghetti sauce, and old books, like a library where sweaty men go to cook spaghetti.
- ☐ The guy sitting next to me on the plane was so fat, when he yawned, the oxygen masks dropped.
- ☐ Gravy so thin that it can be served as a beverage
- ☐ It was so dark, it was like three midnights in a jug.
- ☐ She's seen more beds than a hotel maid
- ☐ They are so Catholic, they only eat sprinkled doughnuts.
- ☐ Like the captain of the Hindenburg asking "Do you smell gas?"
- ☐ Looks like you've been sleeping outside on rocks
- ☐ As coordinated like fingers on a hand
- ☐ Shaking like a fat hooker on a cold night
- ☐ Hair growing out of my nose like marijuana plants
- ☐ Hotter than a matchhead
- ☐ As polite as pie
- ☐ He was all over it like moss on a Mississippi tree stump.
- ☐ I sweat like iced tea in August.

- ☐ That carpenter is such a perfectionist the he puts a level on his level.
- ☐ Floating like a table at a séance
- ☐ Soaked to the skin
- ☐ Like picking dog poo up using a plastic bag—You know you have poo in your hands, but you're not freaking out
- ☐ Like having a cricket in your room that you can't find
- ☐ We go together like peanut butter and ladies.
- ☐ My date was making me spend money like I had a tree in the back yard.
- ☐ Like seeing a nun's hair under her veil, it takes away the mystery of it.
- ☐ I feel like I just kicked a kitten, albeit a filthy one.
- ☐ More confidence than George Clooney at a singles bar.
- ☐ The dull stare of a dairy cow
- ☐ He was hanging on like a loose tooth.
- ☐ Her tongue was soft and warm like a fleece jacket.
- ☐ Some church songs seem longer than dental school.
- ☐ Tighter than bark on a tree
- ☐ So much jewelry, she looked like a Tijuana shopping cart
- ☐ As easy as pie
- ☐ A town so small it's just a wide spot in the road.
- ☐ Villagers so hungry, the were eating next spring's seeds
- ☐ His blue jeans looked as though they were removed from a victim of a car accident.
- ☐ He's so dull, she's collected her life insurance.
- ☐ He (or she) sweats like a man.
- ☐ As comfortable as a flannel shirt
- ☐ Smells like a chicken coop on fire, stuffed with dead dogs
- ☐ As quick as a wink
- ☐ The gossip wasn't as good as a cup of curdled spit.
- ☐ The scented candle the size of a fire hydrant

☐ She's so ugly that she could run nude though a lumberjack camp without any fears.

☐ Mean enough to stomp on a chicken

☐ That corporation is so rich that it hires swans to swim in the pond at corporate headquarters.

☐ Tarantula-grade nose hair

3. Weird and/or Quirky Things

Every now and then Uncle Boogs would spout out something totally from the blue, or use an old phrase in a new context. Sometimes the phrase made no sense at all and I would give him a funny look. If he would look back at me the same way, that's when something inside of me said, "You better write that one down."

- ☐ Higher-order skills
- ☐ Porridge
- ☐ Psychotechnologies
- ☐ Hypersleep
- ☐ Dixie cup of nickels
- ☐ Leather-headed ideas
- ☐ One-hour photo finishing
- ☐ Betty Crocker, Alabama
- ☐ Rumpus room
- ☐ King James Bible-length menu
- ☐ The gospel of relaxation
- ☐ National Federation of Associations
- ☐ A Jerry Lewis conniption fit
- ☐ Liquid evil
- ☐ Courageous avatars
- ☐ Kindred spirits
- ☐ Tap water
- ☐ Sergeant-in-a-box

☐ Blackboard jungle
☐ Major heartburn
☐ The Valley of Holiness
☐ Dry gripes
☐ Man trance
☐ Whiskey kegs
☐ Deep-fried coleslaw
☐ Vulgar hand gestures
☐ Sardine liquor
☐ The lost Chipmunks Tapes
☐ Powerful skills
☐ Spiral eyes
☐ Duct tape imprisonment
☐ The Vietnam veteran hundred-yard stare
☐ Institute for the Very, Very Nervous
☐ K-Mart's blue light special on bib overalls and fishing lures
☐ Spine tingler
☐ Morning Edition with Bob Edwards
☐ Pixelated photo on an ID
☐ Acid test
☐ Two rocks the size of dinosaur nuts
☐ The Bent Propeller Bar
☐ Shoes made of dead reptiles
☐ Hassock and davenport
☐ Complimentary pairings
☐ A fine TOOTH comb
☐ Belt buckles and broomsticks
☐ Geriatric Park
☐ Relevant issues
☐ Nut clusters
☐ Mental pain and anguish
☐ Tiddlywinks
☐ Lightning in a bottle

- ☐ A singing sonogram
- ☐ Federal witness protection plan
- ☐ We asked real people this question…
- ☐ A busted accordion
- ☐ Flip-up contacts, needed only for reading
- ☐ Hey…Man Boobs
- ☐ Arlo Guthrie
- ☐ Cigarette tree
- ☐ New patient fee
- ☐ A dead deer was strapped to the wing of the plane
- ☐ Golf clap
- ☐ Tunnel vision
- ☐ Mexican standoff
- ☐ A cast iron stomach and an asbestos tailpipe
- ☐ Psychoceramics…The study of crack pots
- ☐ Hot Sheets Motel
- ☐ Noodle in a haystack
- ☐ Police blotter
- ☐ Ring of Fire chili
- ☐ A science of exceptions
- ☐ The alchemist's laboratory
- ☐ A Daisy Duke convention
- ☐ Shortwave radio
- ☐ Solar powered sunlamp
- ☐ "No Insurance…" bumper sticker
- ☐ Fun-size
- ☐ The Holy Grail
- ☐ Rocket Science
- ☐ Skeleton keys
- ☐ Marshmallow rock
- ☐ The Tally-ho Tavern
- ☐ Service agreement for an extension cord
- ☐ Red-hot coals

- ☐ Asbestos in your Kool-Aid for breakfast
- ☐ The Chernobyl Training Department
- ☐ Testosterone poisoning
- ☐ The "Spotlight" (i.e. The Rock and Roll Spotlight, or training spotlight, or trout fishing spotlight)
- ☐ Shoestring budget
- ☐ The Rob Petrie Dish
- ☐ Gremlin, Montego, Javelin, Pacer
- ☐ Mental health hazards
- ☐ Syringe music
- ☐ Theater of the mind
- ☐ Pigment of my imagination
- ☐ Nowsville
- ☐ A three-way light bulb for the refrigerator
- ☐ Bag of door knobs
- ☐ Rubber-tipped melon balls
- ☐ Old Spice, Hai Karate, Jade East, English Leather
- ☐ Tribal gene pool
- ☐ The wrath of happiness
- ☐ Pork chops and fried onions
- ☐ Construction paper
- ☐ Time lapse photography of a rotting sparrow
- ☐ A Charles Nelson Riley lunchbox with a Rip Taylor thermos
- ☐ The walk of shame
- ☐ The concealed weapons drill team
- ☐ Diphthong
- ☐ Kittens Without Whiskers Fund
- ☐ Phantom limb
- ☐ Dinner music for people who aren't very hungry
- ☐ You figure the tip, I'm no Bowmar Brain
- ☐ A climate of disrespect
- ☐ Music to watch girls by
- ☐ Goose-skin (goose bumps)

- ☐ Fish stick factory
- ☐ Thoughtful insults
- ☐ Loud Mouth Lime (you remember Funny Face Drink Mix)
- ☐ Low-stimulus environment
- ☐ Matching grant money
- ☐ Amish guy in Circuit City
- ☐ Red Cheek, Arkansas
- ☐ Beer and skittles appetizer
- ☐ Half-baked ideas
- ☐ Brass tacks
- ☐ Nirvana
- ☐ Deviled eggs
- ☐ The Lazy Zion ranch, Lutheran dude ranch
- ☐ My pre-syphilitic period
- ☐ Brail keys for drive up ATMs
- ☐ Their Christmas tree was decorated with Shell No-Pest strips.
- ☐ Fruit float
- ☐ Keyboard plaque
- ☐ Burned to a cinder
- ☐ A culture of secrecy, complacency, arrogance, and negligence
- ☐ Tweezers
- ☐ Tehachapi Glee Club
- ☐ Tarot cards
- ☐ Skeletons in my closet
- ☐ A peace treaty with England
- ☐ Chicken in a biscuit
- ☐ imasucker.com
- ☐ Bobby pin
- ☐ Do-it-yourself aluminum stomach pump
- ☐ Walrus Gumboot

- ☐ Muscle beach
- ☐ The Saps Convention
- ☐ A snowstorm of Styrofoam litter
- ☐ Waterfront flophouse
- ☐ A radish carved to look like a first trimester fetus
- ☐ Lines of cleavage
- ☐ Inferiority complex
- ☐ Ladies' Clubs
- ☐ Deep cover
- ☐ The Bin Laden Letters
- ☐ The Center of Advanced Hindsight
- ☐ Electronic sweatshop
- ☐ A blowtorch of a radio signal
- ☐ Myths and misconceptions
- ☐ Potter's field
- ☐ The curse of a serpent's bite
- ☐ A dirty hovel unfit for a dog
- ☐ Mutual Admiration Society
- ☐ Powder milk briskets
- ☐ Fruit salad fling
- ☐ Mentally double-jointed
- ☐ Big Rocks
- ☐ Guff
- ☐ Sheepshank, Missouri
- ☐ A recipe for paralysis
- ☐ One-point-two Gigawatts
- ☐ Pencil skirt
- ☐ Nut picks
- ☐ Sandcastles hit by a tsunami
- ☐ Low-wattage depression
- ☐ Coconut water
- ☐ Belly aches
- ☐ Flop house

- [ ] The salmon throw (Olympic event)
- [ ] English Leather, made from real Englishmen
- [ ] The annual toast-and-jelly breakfast
- [ ] Barnacles on the ship
- [ ] A highline management style
- [ ] King Brisket Flour Hour
- [ ] Spam Stroganoff with Hubba-Hubba Sauce
- [ ] Crossed fingers
- [ ] Smug certainty
- [ ] A drop of resin
- [ ] Fish-eye
- [ ] Circus of the Stars
- [ ] Lockstep
- [ ] Courtyard of the eggheads
- [ ] Moby Dick…the disease
- [ ] Junkyard dog
- [ ] Skunk's arm pit
- [ ] Parting gifts for our contestants
- [ ] American duct tape council
- [ ] Square root of an imaginary number
- [ ] Flying saucers
- [ ] Critical mass
- [ ] Fish sticks
- [ ] DEFCON 3
- [ ] Urban cowpie
- [ ] A Rolex bar-b-que grill
- [ ] A scorpion dance
- [ ] Brain fever
- [ ] Dobermans wearing gold chains and "Free OJ" tee shirts
- [ ] Fish stick au gratin
- [ ] Horrific psychological experiments
- [ ] Fascination of the forbidden
- [ ] Sister Hail Mary Boarding School and Kennel

- [ ] TV remote as belt ornament
- [ ] Lime Jell-O marshmallow walnut jubilee
- [ ] Black and Decker aftershave lotion
- [ ] Hostess Fruit Pies
- [ ] Whipping post
- [ ] Home-brew
- [ ] The running of the hill-women
- [ ] The First and Last Baptist Church of Mayberry
- [ ] Celebrity Bowling
- [ ] Arch supports, from St. Louis
- [ ] Tater Tot soufflé
- [ ] A cake that Charlie tuna popped out of
- [ ] Weak vital signs
- [ ] Vacuum-packed
- [ ] Miracle at Lourdes
- [ ] Summer squash
- [ ] Worthy objectives
- [ ] Hair made of rayon
- [ ] Dorothy's ruby slippers
- [ ] Easily-digestible bite-sized nuggets of information
- [ ] Fried yack
- [ ] Sea cow
- [ ] A stinger cocktail
- [ ] Giggles
- [ ] Tattoos of guys robbing a gas station
- [ ] Mudflap girl
- [ ] Kumquats
- [ ] Chateaubriand
- [ ] The Saddle Rash Bar
- [ ] Four-slice toaster
- [ ] Chatterbox Café
- [ ] The clapper
- [ ] Sweat lodge

- ☐ Industrial-strength janitor in a drum
- ☐ Sensitivity sessions
- ☐ Gemstones
- ☐ Pithy remarks
- ☐ Horehound balls
- ☐ Missile Parade
- ☐ Bill's PMS Shelter for Men
- ☐ Nursing home bathtub where industrial sandpaper, glued to the bottom, prevents slippage
- ☐ Jumper cables for your pacemaker
- ☐ Optical delusions
- ☐ Mad cow
- ☐ Teen Beat Magazine
- ☐ Shake and Bake
- ☐ Ice Station Zebra
- ☐ A set of salad bowls that all say *Cool Whip*
- ☐ Birth pains
- ☐ A prune Danish
- ☐ Jumping jack
- ☐ B-framed house
- ☐ Girl farts
- ☐ The hammer throw
- ☐ A museum where they have all the arms and hands of statues of other museums
- ☐ Little Friskies
- ☐ Mock-nausea
- ☐ Plain vanilla anything
- ☐ This is not the hill I want to die on
- ☐ "Happy Birthday Banner"
- ☐ Skullduggery
- ☐ Grandiose omnipotence
- ☐ Price of the pudding
- ☐ The Fisherman's Porch, the restaurant

- ☐ Casper-white milk toast
- ☐ The sporting lexicon used to describe hail size
- ☐ Musical pursuits
- ☐ Bring An Angry White Male To Work Day
- ☐ Monte Carlo Night for Gambler's Anonymous
- ☐ Short shrift
- ☐ Skid row
- ☐ Secret sauce
- ☐ A lesbian convent school
- ☐ Spooky paradoxes
- ☐ Toxic features
- ☐ Kung Fu Grip
- ☐ Golden underwear shredder
- ☐ Twigs and berries for breakfast
- ☐ Bean dip
- ☐ National Fear Index
- ☐ Unmuzzle your wisdom
- ☐ The Land of Honahlee
- ☐ Taco Bell, the Mexican phone company
- ☐ Fog blinded
- ☐ High-water mark
- ☐ Cerebral cortex
- ☐ The WHOLE enchilada
- ☐ Tract mansions
- ☐ Thermal nuclear war
- ☐ Kenner Easy Bake Oven
- ☐ Razor-sharp reflexes
- ☐ Intellectual tapestry
- ☐ Dirty tricks
- ☐ A dog without a country
- ☐ Yasgur's Farm
- ☐ Murgatroyd
- ☐ Throat culture

- ☐ Scooter pies
- ☐ Muskrat Love
- ☐ Transcendental concepts
- ☐ The drama of sorority life
- ☐ A photon
- ☐ A nuclear-powered ice cream machine, no melt downs
- ☐ The third rail at work—you touch it and you die
- ☐ Use a cheater bar on hammers
- ☐ Five-star bitching
- ☐ The least-dirty of quick ways
- ☐ Kon-tiki
- ☐ The Beer Truck Theory
- ☐ Jiu-jitsu
- ☐ Turkey Creek
- ☐ Baba ghanoush
- ☐ A bushel of hog testicles
- ☐ Industrial strength humidity
- ☐ Falsification of character
- ☐ Meatballs
- ☐ Ouija board
- ☐ A service warranty for batteries
- ☐ Weiner fondue
- ☐ The House of Mirth
- ☐ Virtual objects
- ☐ Vocabulator builder-upper
- ☐ Smart-assery
- ☐ Sinus Pain Institute
- ☐ Skipper and Midge
- ☐ A road-kill coat
- ☐ Metric vise grips
- ☐ The cowl of a monk
- ☐ Liar's society: "We like it and we do it well."
- ☐ A pair of hairy butcher's arms

- [ ] The Aurora borealis
- [ ] Shameless self-promotion
- [ ] Sherlock Holmes, the subdivision
- [ ] The planet Shirley
- [ ] My rendezvous with dementia
- [ ] Starter marriage
- [ ] A pitter bill to swallow
- [ ] Meat Robot (husband with a cell phone at a grocery store)
- [ ] A quilted infant support bag
- [ ] Kwanzaa
- [ ] Chair lift for cross-country skiers
- [ ] McDonald's gift certificates
- [ ] Cosmoline
- [ ] The dayroom at juvie
- [ ] A beaker of firewater
- [ ] Crazy zone
- [ ] Underdog super-energy pills
- [ ] La Paz, Bolivia
- [ ] Squadron of blackbirds
- [ ] A sexual attraction to Wilma Flintstone
- [ ] A costly game of chicken
- [ ] Three-hour crucible of pain and agony (three-hour tour)
- [ ] Weasel Creek, Wyoming
- [ ] Tone deaf
- [ ] Pet the Tame Deer Park
- [ ] Sandpaper gin
- [ ] Tuna puffs
- [ ] Tomato soup cake
- [ ] The mother tongue
- [ ] Cupcake wars
- [ ] Smuppy (Saving Mostly Until Past Parenting Years)
- [ ] Pigeon tartare
- [ ] Stomach implants

- [ ] Premedicated murder
- [ ] A giant meatloaf on *Let's Make a Deal*
- [ ] Squeeze cheese
- [ ] After he ran away, his photo took all four sides of the milk carton.
- [ ] Parachute pants
- [ ] Dixie Hotel
- [ ] A phaser
- [ ] Brainstem issues
- [ ] Non-toxic chalk
- [ ] Karate chop
- [ ] Irregular verb
- [ ] South Overshoe, Minnesota
- [ ] Heebie-jeebies
- [ ] Vatican toiletries—Pope on a Rope
- [ ] Pucker factor
- [ ] Mint doughnuts
- [ ] Snide remarks
- [ ] Not even a half a thimble of knowledge
- [ ] Deeper senses of the mind
- [ ] Reality contortion field
- [ ] Monkey matter
- [ ] Scooters up on blocks in remote areas of cruise ships
- [ ] St. Elmo's fire
- [ ] Riot gun
- [ ] Pussyfoot
- [ ] The Ovular Office
- [ ] Art heist
- [ ] A wicker wheel chair and leather leg braces
- [ ] The trailer park had an above ground hot tub.
- [ ] Flagship
- [ ] Soul patch
- [ ] Dilly Bars

- ☐ Primary male characteristic
- ☐ Poppycock
- ☐ Side of lima beans
- ☐ A double-wide beauty
- ☐ Sneakers
- ☐ Secondhand stupidity
- ☐ Kettle of fish
- ☐ A climate of disrespect
- ☐ Tie a double upside-down, cross-eyed fisherman's knot behind your back, with your eyes closed.
- ☐ Sugar Smacks
- ☐ Shaggy-dog story
- ☐ Oprahesque self-help Kool-Aid
- ☐ Denim hot pants
- ☐ An oh-no second
- ☐ Dry throat syndrome
- ☐ Dippity-do
- ☐ Restaurants where the menus are coated in plastic and a family member is chained to the cash register
- ☐ Square root of a negative number
- ☐ The dead grass theory
- ☐ Breast milk cheese
- ☐ Zombie containment unit
- ☐ Critical-man life insurance policy
- ☐ Penmanship
- ☐ Panty Check
- ☐ Law of diminishing astonishment
- ☐ Make-you-want-to-call-the-cops music
- ☐ Plug nickel
- ☐ Home for the uncertain
- ☐ State Department of Regulations
- ☐ SELL (red light on a dashboard)
- ☐ Female solidarity

- ☐ Cop out
- ☐ Side-splitting
- ☐ Chocolate cake and onion ring diet
- ☐ Toxic lunacy
- ☐ A Ken Burns documentary on Ken Burns
- ☐ Litmus test
- ☐ The mid-life crisis store
- ☐ Bio break
- ☐ Sock puppets
- ☐ Cherokee Nation
- ☐ Bitch cakes
- ☐ Smothered Meatballs
- ☐ Post-life crisis
- ☐ Dork City
- ☐ Carl's School of Cosmetology and Meat Cutting
- ☐ Whining feature
- ☐ Robo-help
- ☐ Petered out
- ☐ Decaf Prozac
- ☐ Mind bender
- ☐ State of the art, country of the art
- ☐ Black shoals valuation
- ☐ Coffee rings
- ☐ TripTik
- ☐ Whine and cheese party
- ☐ A dimly lit Quonset hut in Nam
- ☐ Shiny objects
- ☐ Football, basketball, and a highball
- ☐ Turkey condom bayou
- ☐ A fuzzy mustache
- ☐ Dave's School of Table Tennis
- ☐ A juice glass of gin
- ☐ Miracle fiber

- ☐ Smashmouth politics
- ☐ Tacit salute
- ☐ Lake Woebegone
- ☐ The sword of Damocles
- ☐ Pimple cream
- ☐ Beg-a-thon
- ☐ Peaceful slumber
- ☐ Fusion in a jar
- ☐ A room in the basement with a bean bag chair
- ☐ Doggie doughnut
- ☐ Zero-sum game
- ☐ Rhetorical questions
- ☐ The curse of a serpent's bite
- ☐ The Zapruder film
- ☐ Cowboy wisdom
- ☐ Tofu mint chip ice ream
- ☐ Parade of lunacy
- ☐ Gadgetry
- ☐ A Mary Tyler Moore hat-toss
- ☐ Scenarios from hell
- ☐ The global village
- ☐ Dipsy Doodles
- ☐ The Battle of Hastings
- ☐ A caricature of a caricature
- ☐ A black art
- ☐ Kipper
- ☐ Lizard men
- ☐ Pudding skin
- ☐ Livermush sandwich with mustard
- ☐ Monkey shine
- ☐ Breakneck speed
- ☐ Guilty conscience
- ☐ Three-point landing

- ☐ Salmon throwing contest
- ☐ Prince Charles Syndrome ("Will I ever get to be king?")
- ☐ A Magoo-like blur
- ☐ Dog cussing
- ☐ Rhetorical statements
- ☐ Shortening bread
- ☐ An X-rated tome
- ☐ A Bowie spoon
- ☐ Delicate lavender scented hair
- ☐ Fidelity to the objectives
- ☐ The battle of Bull Run
- ☐ Macarena Monday
- ☐ The milk of human kindness
- ☐ The cut of one's jib
- ☐ Brain Trust
- ☐ Herpes, Kansas
- ☐ A chafing dish
- ☐ Alms houses
- ☐ Alligator lizards
- ☐ Turbo kiss
- ☐ A net that stops the tuna and lets the dolphins through
- ☐ International House of Computer-Based Training
- ☐ Slime on toast
- ☐ Butt soup
- ☐ Performance-enhancing software
- ☐ The genetic pool
- ☐ A Master's in screwing up
- ☐ The stories behind the stories
- ☐ Operating room humor
- ☐ Cold cuts
- ☐ Yuppie food coupon (twenty-dollar bill)
- ☐ A vaccination against foolishness
- ☐ Neckbeards

- ☐ The toast department of the supermarket
- ☐ My celebrated career
- ☐ Beta blocker
- ☐ DDT
- ☐ A tinker's damn
- ☐ Dirty bomb
- ☐ Coupon on the airsick bag for film developing
- ☐ The Pottery Barn
- ☐ Bikini Wednesday
- ☐ Parking for the emotionally handicapped
- ☐ Pavlov's slobbering dog
- ☐ Nuggets of information
- ☐ Dirty jobs
- ☐ A cologne called *Hot Pockets,* microwave before applying
- ☐ Mumps
- ☐ Geiger counter
- ☐ Ground zero
- ☐ The Nervous Hospital
- ☐ Exploding pies
- ☐ *Tighten up* (the song)
- ☐ Amino acid
- ☐ Mysteries of the trade
- ☐ The skin of my teeth
- ☐ Franklin mint (the candy)
- ☐ Death rattle
- ☐ On the bleeding edge
- ☐ Campfire stories
- ☐ The way-back machine
- ☐ Helter Skelter
- ☐ A timely topic
- ☐ Juvie
- ☐ Western Omelet…with a Marlboro cigarette crushed on top

- ☐ Tide marks
- ☐ Nicene Creed
- ☐ Spider monkeys
- ☐ Incoming choppers
- ☐ Hanky-panky
- ☐ Choctaw Ridge
- ☐ Barbie Dream House
- ☐ Double Dutch
- ☐ Tsunami debris
- ☐ Hall pass
- ☐ A Columbo starter kit
- ☐ A voice technology
- ☐ Meow Mix
- ☐ Yeoman's effort
- ☐ Bugle Boy jeans
- ☐ Brain growth
- ☐ Head-banging music
- ☐ Political parties that blur class lines
- ☐ Fur-licking instincts
- ☐ A guerrilla war
- ☐ Twinkies
- ☐ Dain Bramage
- ☐ Milk and arsenic
- ☐ Brylcreem
- ☐ Incense and wind chimes
- ☐ The dirt road of disinformation
- ☐ Senility implants
- ☐ Massive sobs and snot bubbles
- ☐ Piggly Wiggly store
- ☐ Soothing balm
- ☐ International Salt and Pepper Association
- ☐ The Dixie Hotel
- ☐ A 175-pound skin-tag

☐ Patrol boys
☐ Eight-pound seagull
☐ Technology Shop
☐ Packets of duck sauce from the 70s
☐ The Shroud of Memphis
☐ Congealed salad
☐ The Bozone layer
☐ A king's ransom
☐ The statue of the Unknown Norwegian
☐ Natural wisdom
☐ Chinese water torture
☐ Modus operandi
☐ Neuroplasticity
☐ A cheap cardboard suitcase

4. Philosophical Reflections

Philosophy (/fə'läsəfē/): the study of ideas about knowledge, truth, or the nature and meaning of life.
Reflection (/rĭ-flĕk'shən/): serious thought or consideration.

Every time Uncle Boogs would get that certain look on his face; you could tell he was pondering life's mysteries. That, or he forgot to take his pills.

- ☐ In a game of losers, there are no winners.
- ☐ The bike ain't yours till there's blood on it, and then it owes you.
- ☐ My father's city has many mansions, condos, and townhouses.
- ☐ Why drink American squirrel whiskey that makes men nutty and climb trees when you can enjoy Scotch instead?
- ☐ Yes, there will be misery, and yes I will be miserable.
- ☐ I am at my best happiness when alone.
- ☐ The truth has no agenda.
- ☐ Discoveries are made by not following directions.
- ☐ Laugh and the whole world laughs with you; Puke and you're on your own.

HAVE YOU EVER STARED INTO A STAR-LADENED SKY? WERE YOU COMPELLED TO THINK DEEP THOUGHTS BUT CAME UP EMPTY HANDED? IDENTIFY SOME OF THESE REFLECTIONS TO GIVE YOUR BRAIN SOMETHING WORTHY TO PONDER. BY THE WAY, YOU ONLY HAVE TWO BEERS LEFT IN THE COOLER.

☐ The person that never has the fortitude to pursue his own dreams will be the first to try and discourage you from pursuing yours.

☐ Being an ugly woman is like being a man: you know you're going to have to work the rest of your life.

☐ Advice after injury is like medicine after death.

☐ Speech is linear, only one word comes out at a time.

☐ My fears have been replaced by reality.

☐ Children these days have a sense that delayed gratification is a punishment worse than spanking.

☐ The last capitalist we shall hang is the one who sold us the rope.

☐ If I had known I was going to live this long, I would have taken better care of myself.

☐ If you think it can't get worse, you're overlooking something.

☐ Patience is merely the art of concealing one's impatience.

☐ It's like perfume, intended to be inhaled and not swallowed.

☐ If none of us is prepared to die for freedom, then all of us will die under tyranny.

☐ Why is it that you never see a baby squirrel?

☐ Teaching is like using a funnel: after a while you've got to quit pouring and let some sink in.

☐ Stolen sweets are sweeter.

☐ A lot of people don't have much to say, and that's fine. The trouble with some of them is you have to listen a long time to find out.

☐ Lounged in the frictionless world I live, all things are possible.

☐ It's not what it could have been, but it's not what it could have been.

☐ In the land of skunks, the man with half a nose is king.

☐ Use it up or wear it out. Make it new or do without.

- At a formal dinner party, the person nearest death should always be seated closest to the bathroom.
- I've got a funny feeling I won't be feeling funny very long.
- Sometimes I wonder why that Frisbee is getting bigger, and then it hits me.
- A closed mouth gathers no feet.
- The best way to make a long story short is to stop listening.
- Give people all day to do something and they'll take all day.
- Life is like a bicycle: in order to keep your balance, you must keep moving.
- If you give a man three crap sandwiches, he's going to have a favorite.
- I started out with nothing and still have most of it left.
- The "Math/Science" salmon who swims upstream is one smart fish.
- Naturals aren't developed, they appear.
- You must believe in yourself when nobody else does, like now.
- Who's to blame for the death? The man who hung the gun on the wall, the man who left the bullet in the chamber, or the man who pulled the trigger?
- Just when you see the light at the end of the tunnel, the roof caves in.
- If a man makes a statement with no woman present, is he still wrong?
- The truth will set you free, but first it will piss you off.
- To err is human, to get rich is divine.
- Everybody wants to go to heaven but nobody wants to die.
- Stolen water tastes sweeter.
- Make it idiot-proof and they'll make better idiots.
- In a world of diarrhea and constipation, it's okay to be a shit sometimes.

☐ If you don't want people to know how stupid you are, keep your mouth shut.

☐ I'm 48 but I should be 49—I was held back a year.

☐ You can't dance at two weddings at the same time.

☐ Show me a good loser and I'll show you a loser.

☐ The day after tomorrow is the third day of the rest of your life.

☐ Years ago, before schools, people had to find smart people and follow them around to get an education.

☐ Nothing is impossible for those who don't have to do it.

☐ A blip on the radar screen of eternity

☐ I lived a golden life, no real tragedies.

☐ The veil of obscurity is a second death.

☐ Those who don't study the past will repeat its errors, those who do will find other ways to err.

☐ All that's necessary for evil to flourish is for good men to ignore and say nothing.

☐ The heart of a fool is in his mouth, but the mouth of a wise man is in his heart.

☐ Some things need to be seen to be believed, other things need to be believed to be seen.

☐ Obedience to law is liberty.

☐ Life is like a tackle box. Don't mourn the lures you lost yesterday, and don't worry about the lures you'll lose tomorrow.

☐ I married Miss Right. I just didn't know her first name was Always.

☐ Kissing my husband was like kissing an ashtray. Whenever he goes out of town, and I miss him, I buy a pack of smokes.

☐ Work expands so as to fill the time available for its completion.

☐ The line of demarcation between education and propaganda is a fine one.

- ☐ I will fight no more forever.
- ☐ Ancient wisdom, passed father to son
- ☐ Until you have the courage to lose sight of the shore, you will not know the terror of being forever lost at sea.
- ☐ Regular naps prevent old age, especially when you take them while you're driving.
- ☐ Errors will be made and others will be blamed.
- ☐ If we only wait for the wound to scab over before deep healing, we will only injury it again.
- ☐ The answers are written in the shifting sands of my mind.
- ☐ Two words come to mind...coo coo ca choo.
- ☐ Ignorance is as powerful as knowledge.
- ☐ You can observe a lot by just watching.
- ☐ If it's your job to eat a frog, it's best to do it first thing in the morning. And if it's your job to eat two frogs, it's best to eat the biggest one first.
- ☐ Poverty is not a crime.
- ☐ Never use a big word when a little filthy one will do.
- ☐ If no one ever took risks, Michelangelo would have painted the Sistine Chapel floor.
- ☐ Wherever you are, there is Eden.
- ☐ Few secrets last long—either they're too good to keep or not worth keeping anyway.
- ☐ "If you're drinking tonight, take the bus," my old man said. Hell, I can hardly parallel park a car. No way I can park the bus.
- ☐ The first step in forgiveness is realizing that the other person is an idiot.
- ☐ A riddle wrapped in an enigma, inside a conundrum
- ☐ Sex is like air, it isn't important until you don't get it.
- ☐ You can always tell the ignorant person in an argument—he's the one yelling the loudest.
- ☐ I'm always sure, I'm not always right.

☐ There are basically two types of people: People who accomplish things and people who claim to have accomplished things. The first group is less crowded.

☐ Performance Zone, where the music, the dance, and the dancers are one.

☐ No matter where you go, there you are.

☐ Nothing like a little experience to upset a theory.

☐ I'll seize the day tomorrow.

☐ You can't buy good teeth in the mail anymore, not even on Amazon.

☐ Nothing so needs reforming as other people's habits.

☐ The best time to relax is when you don't have time to relax.

☐ A day will come when the lion and lamb will lie down together, but the lamb won't sleep much.

☐ Sooner or later the boil needs to be lanced.

☐ The best way to cheer yourself up is to try to cheer somebody else up.

☐ In Springfield, smoking in public buildings is prohibited, so people working at gas stations need to smoke outside.

☐ Sometimes the dogs just don't like the dog food.

☐ Experience is knowing a lot of things you shouldn't do.

☐ Education is the ability to listen to almost anything without losing your temper.

☐ People's needs are shaped by an understanding of what is possible.

☐ If flies didn't like dog shit, what would we do with it?

☐ You can lead a horse to water but a pencil has to be led.

☐ After couple's therapy, you can continue to be as mean to each other as in the past, provided you preface every statement with "I feel."

☐ In fifty years we'll all be chicks.

☐ Work is the darlingest recreation and whomsoever Nature has fitted to love it is armed against care and sorrow.

- ☐ If you want to learn a lot about yourse[l]
  your friends, build a boat.
- ☐ Whatever hits the fan will not be evenly dis[tributed]
- ☐ Procrastination is the thief of time.
- ☐ Naiveté, although a shortcoming in any other situa[tion]
  a prerequisite for adventure. Stupidity can be an out[right]
  asset.
- ☐ Doctors don't save lives, they postpone death.
- ☐ If you were right, I would agree with you.
- ☐ The administration's malevolence may be obstructed by
  its incompetence.
- ☐ Even the darkest hour of your life only lasts sixty minutes.
- ☐ Boredom is God's way of telling you that you're
  wasting time.
- ☐ It is an interesting question, how people would retain
  their relative rank in society if they were divested of their
  clothes.
- ☐ Sometimes I think about the values my parents taught me
  and I get a hernia from laughing so hard.
- ☐ Money can't buy happiness, but it keeps the kids
  in touch!
- ☐ Nobody roots for Goliath.
- ☐ My rod and my reel, they comfort me, St. Peter, 12-pound
  test.
- ☐ If you shoot at the king, you better kill the king.
- ☐ 90% of Millennials would rather lose their wallets or
  purses than lose their cellphones.
- ☐ If you can keep your head while others are losing theirs,
  you don't understand the situation.
- ☐ Everything comes to he who hustles while he waits.
- ☐ If only you'd use your powers for good instead of evil.
- ☐ Lack of money is the root of all evil.
- ☐ When you know better, you need to do better.
- ☐ I used to have a handle on life, then it broke.

nkys: they're really good for
e to your face when you push

tertained than educated.
ow much you love, but by how
ers.
uld he make a noise?
net? "I have read and accepted
this application."
.. my youth when I was arrogant and full of
self-pity.

- ☐ I've tasted death, but I did not swallow.
- ☐ With money in your pocket you are wise and you are handsome and you sing well, too.
- ☐ For a person with only a hammer, all problems look like nails.
- ☐ I hope some animal never bores a hole in my head and lays eggs in my brain, because later, you might think you're having a good idea, but it's just the eggs hatching.
- ☐ All of us are born for a reason.
- ☐ Humility is a luxury only the poor can afford.
- ☐ By simply adding a ponytail, a man can remove most of his credibility.
- ☐ Better living through denial
- ☐ I think that's exactly what I would have said if I were talking.
- ☐ I never take advantage of the poor or virtuous.
- ☐ A good lawyer knows the law, a great lawyer knows the judge.
- ☐ The atom should be a worker and not a soldier.
- ☐ Married men live longer than single men. But married men are a lot more willing to die.
- ☐ If I could have dinner with anyone dead or alive, I'd choose alive.

- Money can't buy happiness, but you can afford to look for it in the best places.
- When you make love for the last time, you don't know you are making love for the last time.
- I may lack understanding, but I do not lack love.
- If your mother and father were both drowning, who would you save?
- Absence of evidence is not evidence of absence.
- Swim either for fun or to save your life; it depends on the clothing you're wearing…a pants-suit, naked…
- Worry gives small things big shadows.
- God answers all our prayers, but sometimes the answer is "no."
- If it isn't broke, don't fix it. If it is broke, leave it alone, you might make it worse.
- If you're nice to an animal it loves you for life. If you're nice to a person, who the hell knows what's going to happen.
- Do you not know that I'm a woman, and that whenever I think, I speak?
- Do the right thing. It will gratify some people and astonish the rest.
- Learn through the experience of pain.
- Public radio people aren't happy about anything.
- Whistle away your sadness.
- We are only young once, but we can be immature indefinitely.
- When they pass the law outlawing gravity, people won't start floating to the ceiling.
- America is a country which produces citizens who will cross the ocean to fight for democracy, but won't cross the street to vote.
- If you have ever been hanged, you usually stay away from rope.

☐ If no one is willing to die for freedom, we will all die of tyranny.

☐ Get your facts first, then distort them as you please.

☐ If you continue to what you've always done, you'll continue to get what you've always gotten.

☐ Even a melon grown in the shade eventually ripens.

☐ Therapy helps, but screaming obscenities is cheaper.

☐ Focus on the forest and not the trees.

☐ When arguing with a stupid person, be sure he's not doing the same.

☐ Instead of fixing the toaster, learn to like burned toast.

☐ Whatever you are…be a good one.

☐ I may be old, but I'm stupid.

☐ Money can't buy happiness, but poverty isn't fun either.

☐ Life is unnecessarily complicated.

☐ The person who toots his own horn will have people running out of the way.

☐ A university the team can be proud of.

☐ Most people are about as happy as they make up their minds to be.

☐ That snowflake should not feel responsible for the avalanche, but it does.

☐ By and large, language is a tool for concealing the truth.

☐ Sometimes a cigar is just a cigar.

☐ If the volume of your radio is too high it may annoy your neighbors. But there are many other ways to annoy your neighbors too.

☐ For all the right reasons, she did the wrong things.

☐ Light at the end of the rainbow.

☐ No matter how bad things are, you can always make them worse.

☐ A baby born in a prison does not know that a toilet should not be in the same room as the bed.

☐ Smokers are thinner than most, two to a casket.

- ☐ Compounding interest is the blunt instrument of the retirement toolbox.
- ☐ Amnesia and ignorance are key strategies for this plan's success.
- ☐ Done is better than good.
- ☐ The amount of computing to be done expands until it fills the available capacity.
- ☐ Some days you're the bug and some days you're the windshield.
- ☐ Sticks and stones can really put a deep scratch in the coffee table.
- ☐ The sap of the heart dries up with age.
- ☐ Why is it that if you take a nap in a house where there's a woman, you wake up with a blanket on you?
- ☐ Why does the sun shine in the day when you need it most at night?
- ☐ There'll be a day when there will be no more tomorrows.
- ☐ Start every day off with a smile and then get over it.
- ☐ No one ever went broke saving money.
- ☐ Roller skate on ice and travel faster than light.
- ☐ Beauty is only skin deep, but ugly goes straight through.
- ☐ Romance never goes unpunished.
- ☐ When love and skill work together, expect a masterpiece.
- ☐ When people treat you like they don't care, believe them.
- ☐ Live each day like it is your last, with a lot of crying and whimpering.
- ☐ The question behind the question
- ☐ If you tell the truth, you don't have to remember anything.
- ☐ Children have never been good at listening to their elders, but they have been very good at imitating them.
- ☐ Death is my only friend.
- ☐ If you get to heaven before I do, drill a hole and pull me through.

- ☐ Go out and discover the vast disinterest of the world.
- ☐ A house fire is not an emergency to the fire department.
- ☐ Never alienate the old guard.
- ☐ Call no man happy, until he is dead.
- ☐ I thought I wanted a career…turns out I just wanted paychecks.
- ☐ Going to sea is very much like going to jail, but with the added risk of being drowned.
- ☐ There's nothing more deceptive than an obvious fact.
- ☐ Patience is what you have when there are too many witnesses.
- ☐ People born to be hanged are safe in the water.
- ☐ Two different fingers pointing at the same moon
- ☐ You're more likely to die in a terrible accident than in a wonderful accident.
- ☐ If I had eight hours to chop down a tree, I'd spend seven hours sharpening the axe.
- ☐ Beauty is in the behind of the holder.
- ☐ Deaf ears vs. ears that will not hear
- ☐ Some people are alive simply because it's against the law to kill them.
- ☐ The road is made by walking.
- ☐ If it weren't for this pain in the ass, I'd have no sensation at all.
- ☐ Life is too serious to be taken seriously.
- ☐ Absolute power will corrupt absolutely.
- ☐ Jimmy crack corn and I don't care. What kind of attitude is that?
- ☐ "If you can't stand the heat, stay out of the nuclear reactor." —A. Einstein
- ☐ You can rest more efficiently by laying down.
- ☐ Never fight ugly people, they have nothing to lose.
- ☐ If you aim at nothing, you'll hit it every time.
- ☐ Thirty years ago you always knew where your phone was.

☐ Somebody has to do something, and it is incredibly pathetic that it has to be me.

☐ The crisis of today is the boring history of tomorrow.

☐ Value in order, opportunity in chaos.

☐ We die as we live.

☐ I'm proud to be paying taxes in the U.S. The only thing is, I could be just as proud for half the money.

☐ 98% of all German Shepherds are dogs.

☐ The children were born nine months and ten minutes apart.

☐ The trouble with the future is that it comes before you're ready.

☐ History doesn't repeat itself, but it does rhyme.

☐ The younger generation can't spell as well, based on the way they was brought up.

☐ Half an egg is better than an empty shell.

☐ If you think nobody cares whether you're alive, try missing a couple of payments.

☐ Getting along like a bad waiter and a cheap tipper

☐ The purpose of war is to kill people, break things, and win.

☐ If you don't know where you're going, any road will take you there.

☐ In the kingdom of the blind, the man with one eye is king.

☐ What is mental illness versus the normal suffering of a difficult life?

5. Slang Vernacular

Slang (/slăng/): Language outside of conventional usage.

Vernacular (/vər-ˈna-kyə-lər/): Language of a people or a national language.

The phrases I've included in this chapter have two prevailing themes: corporate America talk and gangster talk.

One time I asked Uncle Boogs how he got his name. He was rather vague. When I asked Mom, she mentioned that he spent a lot of time with his finger up his nose.

- ☐ Motorcycle rider (organ donor)
- ☐ A real thigh-slapper
- ☐ Situation Room
- ☐ Brown paper plan
- ☐ Cube farm
- ☐ Blinkers (eyes)
- ☐ It is not baked in the cake
- ☐ Suds (beer)
- ☐ Twister to the slammer (the key to the door)
- ☐ Woodpile (xylophone)
- ☐ Sky spark (lightning)
- ☐ Dime note ($10 bill)
- ☐ Scrubbed (aborted)

- ☐ High wattage activities
- ☐ Mouthpiece (spokesman)
- ☐ Brain-locked
- ☐ Backwoods standards
- ☐ Wet your beak
- ☐ Cabbage (money)
- ☐ Earn your chops (gain competence)
- ☐ A bunch of sheep dip
- ☐ Bulldozer (one who sleeps through political speeches)
- ☐ Something has that "smell" to it.
- ☐ Battle tested
- ☐ Overcook something
- ☐ Stock the pond with brown trout.
- ☐ That makeup was put on with a trowel.
- ☐ Cultural change initiatives
- ☐ Stems (legs)
- ☐ Firewater
- ☐ NIMBY (Not In My Back Yard)
- ☐ Cover your bunny
- ☐ Stir (prison)
- ☐ You are not allowed nicotine, caffeine, alcohol, crack cocaine, slippy flippies, jelly stingers, trick sticks, bing bangs, or flying willards.
- ☐ Chest of drawers
- ☐ Discretionary effort
- ☐ Empathy deficit
- ☐ Skin beater (drummer)
- ☐ A cheap suit of ugly
- ☐ He was the first one to roll over
- ☐ Firewalls
- ☐ Shuck fish (clean fish)
- ☐ She was a heat seeking missile.
- ☐ Shizzle (shit)

- ☐ Tee it up with somebody
- ☐ Stand down
- ☐ Iron my shoelaces (go to the bathroom)
- ☐ A blunt weapon
- ☐ I'll give you some moonshine if you show me your jugs.
- ☐ She had a balcony you can read Shakespeare from.
- ☐ Carcinogenic smaze
- ☐ The rainmakers (corporate bosses)
- ☐ Sweetheart of a deal
- ☐ Four-box matrix
- ☐ You always have to stir the turd.
- ☐ Brought before the tribal council
- ☐ Boundary conditions
- ☐ He/she is the canary in our coal mine
- ☐ That idea won't fly.
- ☐ Clams (dollars)
- ☐ Load testing
- ☐ Slush pump (trombone)
- ☐ A puppydine day
- ☐ Creates headwinds for our business
- ☐ That is buggy thinking
- ☐ A disruptive technology
- ☐ The day the omelet hit the fan
- ☐ Virtual sleepiness
- ☐ Applesauce (BS)
- ☐ Advanced thinking
- ☐ Smoking what we're selling
- ☐ Drop anchor
- ☐ Perishable skills
- ☐ A cheerleader in "trouble"
- ☐ I've been flushed from the bathroom of your heart.
- ☐ Go through the fire drills
- ☐ Grease the skids

- ☐ That will cause you to lose your man card.
- ☐ On the lam
- ☐ Shakedown
- ☐ Horse race
- ☐ Shit a 40-foot pipe
- ☐ Bet your hat
- ☐ I just needed to unload my wagon a little.
- ☐ Baked-in
- ☐ Happy hunting grounds
- ☐ A cracked memory chip
- ☐ Skid row
- ☐ Passive losses
- ☐ A deal breaker
- ☐ Puppies
- ☐ Liquid evil (liquor)
- ☐ Toxic assets
- ☐ Gasper (cigarette)
- ☐ Crum crushers (teeth)
- ☐ Stray bullets
- ☐ Offshore
- ☐ Front burner issues
- ☐ We'll burn that bridge when we get to it.
- ☐ Bricks and mortar
- ☐ Bells and smells
- ☐ Too big to fail
- ☐ A fireless cooker (oven)
- ☐ Deadwood
- ☐ After he was run over by a car, they just called him "Pancake Jones."
- ☐ Schlock
- ☐ Haywire
- ☐ Jazz
- ☐ A catch basin

> OFTEN SLANG IS USED TO INTENTIONALLY OBFUSCATE MESSAGES FROM UNINITIATED LAYMEN. NOT UNLIKE THE WAY PARENTS SPEAK PIG LATIN AROUND CHILDREN. OUYAY OWKNAY ATWHAY OTAY ODAY ITHWAY ETHAY ECKBOXESCHAY.

- ☐ Have a little bit of the sacrament (swig of whiskey)
- ☐ Shovel-ready
- ☐ The cigar, my favorite snack food
- ☐ Drop the kids off at the pool
- ☐ Let's double-click on that topic.
- ☐ The Dingo Test...give it to the dog
- ☐ Ancient Chinese secret
- ☐ Applejack
- ☐ Skins (drums)
- ☐ Nursing at the public breast
- ☐ Bravo Sierra (BS)
- ☐ Somebody's hard drive (brain)
- ☐ Demon seed
- ☐ A ship without a wheel
- ☐ The pint of no return
- ☐ Half-loaf solutions
- ☐ Bet your ass
- ☐ Training stick-rate
- ☐ If your eyes linger any longer I'll have to charge rent.
- ☐ I got called into the Chieftain's office.
- ☐ A double whammy
- ☐ Take the cake
- ☐ Move the needle
- ☐ The date went sour
- ☐ A double hernia golf swing
- ☐ Security by obscurity
- ☐ Strong suit
- ☐ Oil my palm
- ☐ Corporate apple carts
- ☐ Ran out of flight deck
- ☐ Cover your bird
- ☐ Banana republic
- ☐ Benchmark

- ☐ The foot is on the other hand
- ☐ He's off the plantation
- ☐ A monkey on your back
- ☐ Bilge water (BS)
- ☐ Talk about something off-line
- ☐ The brain polishing factory
- ☐ A heavy lift
- ☐ That feat required two hands and three truckloads of effort.
- ☐ I was standing at the corner of Coocoo and Nuthead.
- ☐ Shoebox apartment
- ☐ Caressing the twins
- ☐ Walks like a duck
- ☐ Goggles (eye glasses)
- ☐ Start the launch sequence
- ☐ Salt mine
- ☐ One frog skin (a dollar)
- ☐ Canary (female vocalist)
- ☐ Poppycock (nonsense or absurdity)
- ☐ Blabbermouth
- ☐ That smells like ours
- ☐ Sleeping policemen (speed bumps)
- ☐ Buy a loosie (a single cigarette)
- ☐ Rictus grin
- ☐ The corporate fig leaf
- ☐ A double-glove job
- ☐ Black project
- ☐ Chorus tomato (showgirl)
- ☐ Contraband
- ☐ Dog eat dog
- ☐ "You look slinky," I said to my wife at the top of the stairs.
- ☐ Secure the hatch (close the door)

- [ ] Came in throwing heat
- [ ] Table stakes
- [ ] Cheese it
- [ ] Beak (nose)
- [ ] Screwball
- [ ] Easy Sledding
- [ ] Hardpack (snow or cigarettes)
- [ ] So-and-so is in check
- [ ] Bay window
- [ ] Cat (guy)
- [ ] Heat source
- [ ] So-and-so misfired
- [ ] Put the kibosh on something
- [ ] Didn't give a fiddler's fart
- [ ] Homie
- [ ] The code of the hills
- [ ] Bought the farm
- [ ] Knocked off your pins (drunk)
- [ ] Licorice stick (clarinet)
- [ ] A gremlin
- [ ] Snout
- [ ] Stash
- [ ] Chirdlen
- [ ] Burning platform
- [ ] The old school way
- [ ] A skull of mush waiting to be reshaped
- [ ] Completive foot print
- [ ] Damage control
- [ ] Up to snuff
- [ ] A three cushion move
- [ ] Cheese box (school bus)
- [ ] Hit job
- [ ] A case of the vapors

- ☐ Boil it down to the abstract skeleton
- ☐ Cut your chops
- ☐ Close the loop
- ☐ A stripped-down mission-specific version
- ☐ That's the truth Ruth
- ☐ Safe Harbor
- ☐ Bum (bum a ride, bum a cigarette)
- ☐ Spandex, a controlled substance
- ☐ That's only half a loaf
- ☐ Shark repellant
- ☐ This puppy
- ☐ Stress conditions
- ☐ I'm not chopping down the apple tree to build a fruit stand.
- ☐ Down range
- ☐ Eyegasm
- ☐ The blower (the telephone)
- ☐ Snow job
- ☐ A bad day at Black Rock
- ☐ Ping Bill and have him double-click on the budget.
- ☐ Rode hard and put away hot
- ☐ Utilization and development of our human resources
- ☐ Backfill with bodies
- ☐ Mash me a fin (give me five bucks)
- ☐ Dry startup (no lubrication)
- ☐ I got my bacon burned
- ☐ Ship of fools
- ☐ Bill met the bus (died)
- ☐ A whipping boy (a piñata)
- ☐ Cheese and crackers (Jesus)
- ☐ Buddy, you better pump your brakes.
- ☐ Deep yogurt
- ☐ Who's the skirt?

- ☐ Whirl/hurl (vomit)
- ☐ Shanks's pony (using your own legs to motate)
- ☐ So-and-so's body wasn't even cold yet.
- ☐ Sawbones (doctor)
- ☐ A mercy killing
- ☐ Degrade performance
- ☐ Cash money
- ☐ Pulling the boat in the slip (parking the car)
- ☐ A dead cat bounce
- ☐ The day the pacemaker stopped
- ☐ Value-added
- ☐ Prairie dogging (heads pop up on a cube farm)
- ☐ Time to beat the sheets
- ☐ The ratings just jumped 50%, from squat to squat-and-a-half.
- ☐ The acid test
- ☐ Gargoyles (protectors)
- ☐ So-and-so ate the carpet—fuzz, lining, and glue
- ☐ A fat chance
- ☐ Due to circumstances beyond my control…
- ☐ It's your fudge, I'll let you cook it
- ☐ Loose manpower
- ☐ Sourcasm
- ☐ I was quite a dancer back when I had two good stems.
- ☐ Chinese whispers (rumors)
- ☐ Vato (Spanish for "dude")
- ☐ Backwoods Catholicism
- ☐ That dog won't hunt
- ☐ Something went to seed
- ☐ That's your ace in the hole?
- ☐ Knows where the bodies are buried
- ☐ Suppository remarks
- ☐ Will there be a fuse on the line?

☐ When you talk smartly you really sound good.
☐ Poison pills
☐ Biscuit money
☐ Have somebody walk the floors
☐ Drop anchor
☐ I want to butter your muffin
☐ Nickel note (five-dollar bill)
☐ Rock bottom
☐ "I'm not going to fall for that 'stretch goal' crap again."
☐ Heavy lifting
☐ Permahold (on hold forever at a call center)
☐ Grumpies (grown up mature people)
☐ Blow back
☐ Fox paws (faux pas)
☐ Bee in your bonnet
☐ Sub-par output
☐ The dance of succession
☐ A lighting rod
☐ Kneecap (to cripple or limit someone or something)
☐ Armor piercing
☐ Assholiness
☐ I'm taking "old two eye" to the optometrist
☐ Smackers
☐ She's a looker—check out those gams!
☐ A bag of snakes
☐ Shekels (money)
☐ Leaking oil (bleeding)
☐ Sweet talking me like a third cousin
☐ They came to the hanging, two to a mule.
☐ Gin mill
☐ A Sam's Club-size can of whoop-ass
☐ Guy cramps
☐ Ample lips

- A bunch of creeps and bums
- Barn burner
- Strike an arc
- Driving dirty (driving on an expired license or without insurance or registration)
- Veer off course
- Clobber
- Spray and pray training
- Vapor lock (heart attack)
- You can't have your Kate and Edith, too.
- A little pin prick of a place
- A down-hill hike
- Serve as a heat shield
- Chickenshit
- Fluff your pillow (stand up for a break)
- Cross-pollination
- Foghorn (tuba)
- Load shedding
- Gabriels (trumpet players)
- Gabber (mouth)
- Diocese, sort of like a Catholic precinct
- Heat map
- A real bucket of turds
- A house of cards
- Paper storm
- Stiff cheddar (bad luck)
- Loopholes are for people, taxes are for chumps.
- Impact the production environment
- A lizard scorcher (hot day)
- A compelling argument
- Our fingerprints are on that
- A turd in your pocket
- The moment when you earn your bones

- ☐ The ice edge broke again
- ☐ Sharkey
- ☐ The aluminum handshake
- ☐ From the get-go
- ☐ Became an angel (die)
- ☐ A poke in the eye with a sharp shtick
- ☐ A match made in hell
- ☐ That puppet makes a good point
- ☐ A rat fight
- ☐ Going up the hill (getting fired)
- ☐ Beat up the chops (talk, be loquacious)
- ☐ That's what they used to say in juvie
- ☐ I started to drink my own bath water
- ☐ Stewed (drunk)
- ☐ Crippled unit
- ☐ Our black ops agent is "off the reservation."
- ☐ Pay dirt
- ☐ Under the covers
- ☐ Smoke a frajo (smoke a cigarette)
- ☐ The death rattle in his throat
- ☐ The feces will hit the air circulator
- ☐ Bone box (ambulance)
- ☐ A wooden overcoat (a coffin)
- ☐ Testosterone storm
- ☐ I thought you were tits-up (dead).
- ☐ Nose whistle
- ☐ Kick her to the curb of the project
- ☐ Irish confetti (bricks)
- ☐ Fishwrap (newspaper)
- ☐ Collateral damage
- ☐ A person's frame

6. Vocabularyizer

There's nothing special about these words. Any dictionary has them, and goodness knows there are plenty of vocabulary building books written on the subject.

While Uncle Boogs and I would watch Tom Brokaw, he would hear the talking head use an interesting word just beyond his daily lexicon. "Dang, I wish I could remember to use good words like that." Uncle Boogs would say.

After that, I started writing them down as sort of a vocabulary builder-upper study guide.

IF YOU BELIEVE THAT A PERSON IS JUDGED BY THE WIDTH AND DEPTH OF THEIR VOCABULARY, YOU'RE RIGHT. CHECK OFF A FEW FAVORITES AND USE THEM AT DINNER TONIGHT. YOU MIGHT BE ASKED TO STAY FOR BRANDY AND CIGARS.

- ☐ Uncontrolled verbosity—can't stop talking
- ☐ Arcane—understood by few; mysterious or secret
- ☐ Antecedents—the statement contained in the "if" clause of a conditional proposition
- ☐ Matzo—a very sturdy, construction-grade cracker
- ☐ A jaundiced way of looking at things—influenced by bitterness, resentment, or envy
- ☐ Salient—most noticeable or important
- ☐ Ephemeris—a table of data
- ☐ Amidships—in the middle of the ship

- ☐ Draconian—excessively harsh and severe
- ☐ Reticent—not revealing one's thoughts or feelings readily
- ☐ Unremarkable—not particularly interesting or surprising
- ☐ Squalid—extremely dirty and unpleasant, especially as a result of poverty or neglect
- ☐ Duplicit—two-faced, deceitful
- ☐ Sordid—sleazy, seedy, or unsavory
- ☐ Ethos—the spirit of a culture, era, or community as manifested in its beliefs and aspirations
- ☐ Ad hominem—attacking the person rather than their position or argument
- ☐ Disingenuous—not candid or sincere
- ☐ Blame storming—I got nothing
- ☐ Chimpanzify—I don't know, what do you think?
- ☐ Pedantic—someone who is annoying for their attention to minor detail,
- ☐ Debauched—indulging in sensual pleasures to a degree perceived to be morally harmful
- ☐ Quaaludes—methaqualone
- ☐ Inscrutable—impossible to understand or interpret
- ☐ Heady profundities—deep insight
- ☐ Pluvial—of or having to do with rain
- ☐ Effusive—expressing feelings of gratitude, pleasure, or approval in an unrestrained or heartfelt manner
- ☐ Moonstruck—unable to think or act normally, especially because of being in love
- ☐ Enchanting—delightfully charming or attractive
- ☐ Plutocrat—a person whose power derives from their wealth
- ☐ Mandrill—old world monkey
- ☐ Gingerly—in a careful or cautious manner
- ☐ Bindle—a hobo's luggage
- ☐ Pachydermal—big, elephant-sized
- ☐ Flippant—not showing a serious or respectful attitude

- ☐ Fiasco—a thing that is a complete failure, especially in a ludicrous or humiliating way
- ☐ A real treasure trove—just a colorful phrase
- ☐ Linguistic capitulation—relating to language/surrendering to an opponent or demand
- ☐ A comprehensive study of…—just nice words complimenting themselves
- ☐ Machismo—a strong or exaggerated sense of manliness
- ☐ Brogan—a coarse, stout leather shoe reaching to the ankle
- ☐ Tumult—a loud, confused noise, especially one caused by a large mass of people
- ☐ Polyglot—knowing or using several languages
- ☐ Unadorned—not adorned; plain
- ☐ Sanguine—optimistic
- ☐ Drivel—nonsense
- ☐ Apropos—with reference to
- ☐ Brouhaha—a noisy and overexcited reaction to something. And fun to say too
- ☐ Lurid details—ghastly, grisly, gruesome, macabre details
- ☐ Comeuppance—a punishment or fate that someone deserves
- ☐ Salubrious—healthy, wholesome
- ☐ In the aggregate—a whole formed by combining several (typically disparate) elements
- ☐ Cadaver—a corpse
- ☐ Chestnut—an old and moldy joke
- ☐ Crestfallen—sad and disappointed
- ☐ Trope—a figurative or metaphorical use of a word or expression
- ☐ Ham-handed—clumsy or bungling; ham-fisted
- ☐ Diminutive—extremely or unusually small
- ☐ Trajectory—the path followed by a projectile flying
- ☐ Specter—a ghost
- ☐ Implacable—relentless; unstoppable

- ☐ Bifurcate—to cause to divide into two branches or parts
- ☐ Duplicitous—deceitful
- ☐ Technical parameters—just a nice pairing of words
- ☐ Lexicons—the vocabulary of a person or branch of knowledge
- ☐ Culpability—liability
- ☐ Treachery—betrayal of trust; deceptive action or nature
- ☐ Gruntled—pleased, satisfied, and contented
- ☐ Dreadful and hideous—nice words
- ☐ Patrician—aristocrat
- ☐ A fallacious syllogism—"All marathon runners sweat; if you are sweating, you are running a marathon."
- ☐ Buffoonery—behavior that is ridiculous but amusing
- ☐ Ameliorate—make something better
- ☐ Murky—not fully explained or understood, especially with concealed dishonesty or immorality
- ☐ Imbecility—the quality or state of being very stupid or foolish
- ☐ Predicated—found or based on
- ☐ Unsmirched—not dirtied or soiled
- ☐ Pubescent—denoting a person at or approaching the age of puberty
- ☐ Sanctimoniously—showing morally superiority to other people
- ☐ Vicariously—in a way that is experienced in the imagination through the actions of another person
- ☐ Burgeoning competence—simply a nice phrase
- ☐ Venerable—accorded a great deal of respect, especially because of age, wisdom, or character
- ☐ Evoke—bring or recall to mind
- ☐ Simpatico— (a person) likable and easy to get along with
- ☐ Bedraggled—dirty and disheveled
- ☐ Coterie—a small group of people with shared interests or tastes, especially one that is exclusive of other people

- [ ] Bedraggled—dirty and disheveled
- [ ] Battle-hardened—toughened by the experience of battle
- [ ] Candid simplicity—pure and simple
- [ ] Smirchless—not dirtied or soiled
- [ ] Malingering—exaggerate or feign illness in order to escape duty or work
- [ ] Affable—friendly, good-natured, or easy to talk to
- [ ] Resonating (of an idea or action)—meet with someone's agreement
- [ ] Moldering—slow decay or disintegrate, especially because of neglect
- [ ] Ancillary—necessary
- [ ] Manically—behaving like a maniac
- [ ] Ruthful—full of a feeling of pity, distress, or grief
- [ ] Pugnacious—eager or quick to argue, quarrel, or fight
- [ ] Stripling—(see *nipper* or *shaver*)
- [ ] Nipper—a child, especially a small boy
- [ ] Shaver—a young lad
- [ ] Reticent—not revealing one's thoughts or feelings readily
- [ ] Incumbent—necessary, obligatory
- [ ] Pariah—outcast
- [ ] Culpability—responsibility for a fault or wrong; blame
- [ ] Fundamental assumption—nice pairing
- [ ] Copacetic—in excellent order
- [ ] Gesticulate—use dramatic gestures, instead of speaking or to emphasize one's words
- [ ] Diaspora—dispersion of the Jews beyond Israel
- [ ] Vis-à-vis—with regard to
- [ ] Omnipresent—widely or constantly encountered; common or widespread
- [ ] Eschew—deliberately avoid using; abstain from
- [ ] Flagon—a large container for drink
- [ ] Enigma—paradox

- ☐ Sodden—soaked through
- ☐ Spasm—a sudden involuntary muscular contraction or convulsive movement
- ☐ Matriculated—enrolled in a college or university
- ☐ Flummery—empty compliments
- ☐ Bombastic—pompous, blustering, ranting, blathering
- ☐ Jalopy—an old car in a dilapidated condition
- ☐ Flatulence—the accumulation of gas in the alimentary canal
- ☐ Corpus of data—body of data
- ☐ Blather—to talk long-windedly without making very much sense
- ☐ Odious character—extremely unpleasant; repulsive
- ☐ Temerity—excessive confidence or boldness; audacity
- ☐ A smidgeon—just a little
- ☐ Taciturn—cold, aloof
- ☐ Pantaloons—baggy trousers gathered at the ankles
- ☐ Dismal—depressing; dreary
- ☐ Staccato—notes sharply detached or separated from the others
- ☐ Tacit—understood or implied without being stated
- ☐ Turgid—tediously pompous or bombastic
- ☐ Unencumbered—not having any burden or impediment
- ☐ Automagically—automatically and in a way that seems ingenious, inexplicable, or magical
- ☐ Force majeure—unforeseeable circumstances that prevent someone from fulfilling a contract
- ☐ Eschatological—concerned with the final events of history, or the ultimate destiny of humanity
- ☐ Masticating—chewing
- ☐ Ostentatious—characterized by vulgar or pretentious display
- ☐ Obnubilate—to darken or dim
- ☐ Exacerbate—make (a problem, or bad situation) worse

- Cogent—clear, logical, and convincing
- Hubris—excessive pride or self-confidence
- Empirically verifiable—you can really see it
- Excoriating—censure or criticize severely
- Pure conjecture—an opinion formed on the basis of incomplete information
- Mollify—appease the anger or anxiety of (someone)
- Disentangle—free something from an entanglement; extricate
- Omnipresent—widely or constantly encountered; common or widespread
- Proclivity—a tendency to choose or do something regularly
- Rebuffed—reject in an ungracious manner
- Phlegmatic—calm, unflappable
- Ergo—therefore
- Feckless—lacking initiative or strength of character
- Epistle—literary work in the form of a letter or series of letters
- Fiasco—a complete failure, especially in a ludicrous or humiliating way
- Source and summit—just nice words
- Diabolical—characteristic of the Devil, or so evil as to be suggestive of the devil
- Compulsory—required by law or a rule; obligatory
- Blatherskite—a person who talks at great length without making much sense
- Monkish—relating to or characteristic of a monk or monks
- Schadenfreude—delight from other's suffering
- Epithet—nickname/description (Alexander "The Great")
- A shiny pate—a shiny head
- Clavicle—collarbone

☐ Synchronicity—the simultaneous occurrence of events which appear significantly related but have no discernible causal connection

☐ Perfunctory—carried out with a minimum of effort or reflection

☐ Myopic—lacking imagination, foresight, or intellectual insight

☐ Eponymous—named after a particular person

☐ Austerity—extreme plainness and simplicity of style or appearance; "He was noted for his austerity and his authoritarianism."

☐ Polarized—divide or cause to divide into two sharply contrasting groups or sets of opinions or beliefs

☐ Acerbity—sharpness and directness in speech

☐ Irascible personality—easily angered

☐ Portations—things that are carried

☐ Osculate—kiss

☐ Protocol—the official procedure

☐ Blather—long-winded talk with no real substance (see *blatherskite*)

☐ Rascality—mischievous or dishonest behavior or activity

☐ Flinders—small fragments or splinters

☐ A terrible snit—a fit of irritation; a sulk

☐ Metaphysical equivalent—abstract, theoretical, or conceptual equivalent

☐ Extrapolate—the action of estimating or concluding something by assuming existing trends

☐ Grotesquery—repulsively ugly or distorted

☐ Flotsam—the stuff that floats on the top of communal drinking jugs

☐ Troglodyte—caveman

☐ For my own edification—improvement of a person morally or intellectually

☐ Burgeoning—begin to grow or increase rapidly

- [ ] Visceral—relating to deep inward feelings rather than to the intellect
- [ ] Temerity—recklessness
- [ ] Tenacity—persistence
- [ ] Scrimpy—being thrifty or parsimonious; economize
- [ ] Niggly—causing slight but persistent discomfort or anxiety
- [ ] Acrimonious—angry and bitter (acrimonious bastard)
- [ ] Malarias swamp—resembling a swamp with malaria
- [ ] Lummox—a clumsy, stupid person
- [ ] Vignette—a brief evocative description or account
- [ ] Integer—a whole number; a number that is not a fraction
- [ ] A jubilee of pens—bunch of pens in a pocket
- [ ] Prodigious—impressively great in extent, size, or degree
- [ ] Scullery—a small kitchen or room at the back of a house used for washing dishes and other dirty household work
- [ ] Purloined—steal
- [ ] Unscrupulous—having or showing no moral principles; not honest or fair
- [ ] Incapacitated—deprived of strength or power; debilitated
- [ ] Sardonic—grimly mocking or cynical
- [ ] Slapdash—done too carelessly
- [ ] Mitigate—make less severe, serious, or painful
- [ ] Pathogens—a bacterium, virus, or other microorganism that can cause disease
- [ ] Coalition—an alliance for combined action
- [ ] Shenanigans—secret or dishonest activity or maneuvering
- [ ] Nabobs—a person of conspicuous wealth
- [ ] Reprobate—an unprincipled person (often used humorously or affectionately)
- [ ] Omnipresent—widely or constantly encountered; common or widespread
- [ ] Tepid support—lukewarm support
- [ ] Glib—speaking fluently a but insincere and shallow

- ☐ In the ether—something being communicated from place to place; having no precise location, just as a radio broadcast can be heard from many different places
- ☐ Petulance—being childishly sulky or bad-tempered
- ☐ Halcyon—a period of time in the past that was idyllically happy and peaceful
- ☐ Vestals, college of vestals, vestal virgins—chaste, pure
- ☐ Debauchery—excessive indulgence in sensual pleasures
- ☐ Claptrap—absurd or nonsensical talk or ideas
- ☐ Malleability—is the quality of something that can be shaped into something else without breaking
- ☐ Barouche—four-wheeled carriage
- ☐ Habibi—(Arabic) "My love"
- ☐ Bombastic—high-sounding but with little meaning; inflated
- ☐ She was comely—(typically of a woman) pleasant to look at
- ☐ Emasculate—deprive (a man) of his male role or identity
- ☐ Farcical—resembling farce, especially because of absurd or ridiculous aspects
- ☐ Jetsam—unwanted material or goods that have been thrown overboard from a ship and washed ashore
- ☐ Ruthful—full of sorrow; sorrowful; woeful
- ☐ Mercurial temperament—rapid and unpredictable changeableness of mood
- ☐ Coup de grace—death blow
- ☐ Latability—latitude and flexibility
- ☐ Besmirched—damaged the reputation of (someone or something) in the opinion of others
- ☐ Jackassery—the actions of a stupid person
- ☐ Maelstrom—a situation or state of confused movement or violent turmoil
- ☐ Debacle—a sudden and ignominious failure; a fiasco
- ☐ Vagabondish—resembling a person who wanders from place to place without a home or job

- ☐ Fallacious confusion—based on a mistaken belief
- ☐ Incongruently oxymoronic—a figure of speech which is apparently contradictory
- ☐ Unintended consequences—popular phrase
- ☐ Wonky—crooked; off-center; askew (consider *wonkery*)
- ☐ Ipso facto—by that very fact or act
- ☐ Obsequious—obedient to excess
- ☐ A null hypothesis—a hypothesis that there is no significant difference between specified populations
- ☐ Prelude—event serving as an introduction to something more important
- ☐ Irascible—having or showing a tendency to be easily angered
- ☐ Germane—relevant to a subject under consideration
- ☐ Conundrum—a confusing and difficult problem or question
- ☐ Drubbing—a beating; a thrashing
- ☐ Trepidation—a feeling of fear or agitation about something that may happen
- ☐ Capricious—given to sudden and unaccountable changes of mood or behavior
- ☐ Enthalpy—too complicated to explain to a luddite (see *luddite*)
- ☐ Luddite—a person opposed to new technology or ways of working
- ☐ Rapacious—aggressively greedy
- ☐ Catastrophic failures—simple enough
- ☐ Ubiquitous—present, appearing, or found everywhere
- ☐ Caveat—a warning of specific stipulations, or conditions
- ☐ Glyph—a hieroglyphic character or symbol; a pictograph
- ☐ Loquacious—talkative
- ☐ Comely—Pleasant to look at, attractive. Uncle Boogs always thought it was just the opposite. Perhaps he was thinking of homely.

☐ Moronic—very foolish or stupid
☐ Pedantic—unimaginative, dull

7. Rich Literary Phrases

I wouldn't call Uncle Boogs a well-read man. You wouldn't find Dickens or Tolstoy on his bookshelf. His scant "library" existed in the side pocket of his saggy recliner. It included a tattered *MAD Magazine*, a copy of *National Geographic* (the Bali edition) a *TV Guide,* and a Chinese restaurant menu. Regardless, Uncle Boogs did have a good ear for a bouquet of well-crafted words appropriately purposed.

- ☐ Stupefied incredulity and awe
- ☐ It was a cloudy and tempestuous time.
- ☐ A life filled with an abundance of responsibility
- ☐ The lure of adventure
- ☐ Empty bromides
- ☐ Precocious mastery of vulgarisms
- ☐ She arrived home during the small hours of the morning.
- ☐ That comment is offensive to modern ears.
- ☐ The boy is father to the man.
- ☐ Synthetic organization
- ☐ Gratuitous assertions
- ☐ Emphatic laughter
- ☐ Forgive me for intruding on your time and patience.
- ☐ Let me point out…
- ☐ It was a dark and stormy night.
- ☐ A bitter seed was growing inside me.
- ☐ A modest silence is a woman's crown.
- ☐ Political piñatas

- ☐ Lamentable state of affairs
- ☐ A biblical beard
- ☐ The miter has to fit.
- ☐ A glittering generality
- ☐ Buttress your position
- ☐ A maniacal laugh
- ☐ Mutual pragmatism
- ☐ An arrow of starlings
- ☐ Perverse curiosity
- ☐ A blinding headache
- ☐ Mercurial personality
- ☐ Strong and dangerous medicine
- ☐ To my liking
- ☐ Adolescent snickering
- ☐ The winds of war are blowing.
- ☐ A cultural moment
- ☐ To resist the temptation was beyond my strength.
- ☐ A strong wind to sail into…
- ☐ Hold sway over
- ☐ Intellectual whimsy
- ☐ Nineteen miles of muddy road
- ☐ You have a place in my cabinet of human curiosities.
- ☐ Seductive design
- ☐ Repertoire of competencies
- ☐ These sailors had to weather some heavy seas.
- ☐ I will shake you by the hand.
- ☐ Mea Culpa
- ☐ Social conditioning
- ☐ Sunny Mehico
- ☐ All that to say this…
- ☐ Paragon of comeliness
- ☐ The pinch of hard luck
- ☐ A thick body which was thickening

- ☐ The newspapers were soaked with ink covering the scandal.
- ☐ I smell fear
- ☐ Astonished down to my corns
- ☐ Bitter swill
- ☐ An irksome paradox
- ☐ I tell you truly
- ☐ It's been my pleasure and privilege.
- ☐ The patient's bowel movements have become miserly and spontaneous.
- ☐ Thy breath be rude
- ☐ You don't need to strain your imagination.
- ☐ Milk of human kindness
- ☐ We gather to gain strength.
- ☐ A champagne problem
- ☐ Garden variety
- ☐ The boys were adept in their blood sport activities.
- ☐ An elitism based on something other than merit
- ☐ Worthless trumpery
- ☐ I found myself on the pointy end of the spear.
- ☐ A leavening experience
- ☐ A tangle of strangers
- ☐ *Et tu*, Carl?
- ☐ Vestiges of paganism
- ☐ An intense discomfort descended on the room.
- ☐ I assert that…
- ☐ My haze of ignorance
- ☐ I don't mean to give offense.
- ☐ Sagging duplexes
- ☐ You have the virtue and the curse of caring heart.
- ☐ Herculean efforts
- ☐ I offer an explanation, apology, and an excuse.
- ☐ Do you have any reservations about your conclusions?

- ☐ That's intuitive to the most casual observer.
- ☐ So after we danced a few slow songs, I was determined that Steve could revitalize my failing business.
- ☐ Let me say this about that…
- ☐ We need a steady hand at the lever of power.
- ☐ Rip-roaring
- ☐ There is a lot of evidence to refute that.
- ☐ A steadily metastasizing terror threat
- ☐ The horribleness and awfulness of it will never actually be forgotten.
- ☐ "Tell us in your own words."
  "I don't have my own words. I use words that everybody else uses."
- ☐ An alfalfa breeze
- ☐ I'm happy for the pleasure of your company.
- ☐ Virtuous purpose
- ☐ She had a serene and kindly countenance.
- ☐ I do not shear the flock
  I tend.
- ☐ An angry mob of principled citizens
- ☐ The Hercules that vanished the Hydra
- ☐ Thorny problems
- ☐ A smoky laugh
- ☐ A shred of evidence, perhaps just a small shred
- ☐ Rule number one: Never smoke while sleeping. Rule number two: Never refrain while awake.
- ☐ A faded housedress
- ☐ Marbled throughout
- ☐ The shackles of censorship are being loosened around here.
- ☐ The corpus of the trust
- ☐ Turgid, verbose, shapeless, but pregnant with its message
- ☐ The actress has learned her lines well.
- ☐ Moral high ground

- [ ] The altar of low expectations
- [ ] Annoying on a molecular level
- [ ] Covered with boils, wrapped in burlap, sitting in the ashes, and flies on her feet
- [ ] Andy, you are cut of rare cloth, inscrutable and admirable in equal measures.
- [ ] Sodden piece of paper
- [ ] Serious consideration of compelling alternatives
- [ ] The hour of sweet release
- [ ] Wisdom and sensibility
- [ ] A look reserved for the discovery of eight-legged creatures under the sink
- [ ] A Kodak moment
- [ ] Overflowing with the milk of human kindness
- [ ] I turned it over in my mind a long time.
- [ ] I mean that in a very pandering way.
- [ ] In due time
- [ ] The headwinds we face
- [ ] Ruthful vs. ruthless
- [ ] I embraced it and drew it closer.
- [ ] Work is the slow dragging fingernail on the blackboard of life.
- [ ] Spider-infested island nations of the Caribbean
- [ ] I recalled the incident with exacting clarity.
- [ ] A flabby, soft-minded notion
- [ ] Ask of him the privilege of shaking him by the hand.
- [ ] Sadder and wiser
- [ ] The old deluder
- [ ] She was tarred with a brush she didn't deserve.
- [ ] The misunderstanding metastasized into a crisis.
- [ ] Raw antagonism
- [ ] A long winter's nap
- [ ] A clever metaphorical titty pincher

- ☐ Reactionary bourgeois community
- ☐ Logically circular
- ☐ Muddy morass
- ☐ A constellation of attributes
- ☐ The habit was easier to acquire than to get rid of.
- ☐ My poached salmon in white sauce
- ☐ Look longingly at them like they were Victorian street urchins lusting after a hot roll in a bakery window.
- ☐ The soft bigotry of lowered expectations
- ☐ Thank heaven for little girls.
- ☐ You've made some extraordinary claims, and at the risk of sounding realistic…
- ☐ Turn my skeptical eye on…
- ☐ No rancor or malice intended.
- ☐ Don't ruin an apology with an excuse.
- ☐ A laced bosom
- ☐ I submit to you…
- ☐ Everybody joined in, obediently, but not enthusiastically.
- ☐ His voice had a serrated quality to it.
- ☐ I came, I saw, I soiled my pants.
- ☐ A sensible idea
- ☐ Sexually precocious
- ☐ Righteous simplicity
- ☐ The president had a gauzy view of history.
- ☐ Muffled oars
- ☐ Because the account (of the story) is second hand, the telling of it may have been embroidered.
- ☐ The bunks in the old fishing trawler were kippered by the grime and sweat of use by crusty fishermen.
- ☐ An emotional towel snap
- ☐ Tobacco is my sacrament and the smoke is my offering to the spirits.
- ☐ These are deep waters.

- ☐ Domestic headwind
- ☐ From the thinning out the herd category…
- ☐ I'll drizzle you with techniques.
- ☐ The garment starts to unravel
- ☐ Civic virtue
- ☐ The cry of the truly disparate
- ☐ Range of insight, diversity, and specialization
- ☐ A netherworld between fantasy and imagination
- ☐ With no rancor or malice
- ☐ Native features
- ☐ He died with your name in his mouth.
- ☐ A relentless drum beat
- ☐ Long-incubated grudges
- ☐ A Currier and Ives morning
- ☐ Remotely gratified
- ☐ Full-throated apology
- ☐ I'm a little confused by your tactic.
- ☐ Coarse and vulgar
- ☐ Where men sit in air-cooled comfort to medicate themselves against anger and bitterness
- ☐ Tragic set of charms
- ☐ I'm here to tell you…
- ☐ Rancid mind
- ☐ Reckless talk
- ☐ A thin and vigorous body
- ☐ A Cheshire smile
- ☐ Waxing philosophically
- ☐ The student became the master
- ☐ His coat was not overly clean.
- ☐ A large cloud of dark gossip
- ☐ You're dressing the truth in too much costumery. The truth should be dressed in tights.
- ☐ High rhetoric

- ☐ It was a buzzsaw of a job.
- ☐ Pipe smoking facilitates relaxation and objectivity.
- ☐ A thirsty wayfarer
- ☐ Venial aspirations
- ☐ I skid you not.
- ☐ Till death my body chills.
- ☐ Don't do that again lest you…
- ☐ People looked away as though it was the scene of an accident.
- ☐ Blissful ignorance
- ☐ Pure and unadulterated
- ☐ A sleeve full of excuses
- ☐ The winds of change are blowing and storm warning flags are being raised.
- ☐ Part and parcel of…
- ☐ What I'm going to say may sound indelicate…
- ☐ Bottomless pit of needs and wants
- ☐ An onion of layered lies
- ☐ I repent in dust and ashes
- ☐ From the four corners of the earth
- ☐ Tacit knowledge
- ☐ Men of well-sifted reputation
- ☐ He used an inlaid cane to manage his heavy trudge.
- ☐ The room was littered with PEZ wrappers.
- ☐ Beautifully embossed
- ☐ Silence is considered consent.
- ☐ Morbid curiosity
- ☐ Hideously disparaging comments
- ☐ Beyond any conceivable doubt in my mind
- ☐ So-and-so oozed with…
- ☐ If I tell you…
- ☐ The bed is absent of your treasure.
- ☐ What riches would be mine?

- ☐ Crudeness and audacity
- ☐ Selective application of compassion and respect
- ☐ I was smitten with her charms.
- ☐ West Berlin is a bone in my throat.
- ☐ It had a cashmere and hushpuppy feel about it.
- ☐ Do not forget your dying king.
- ☐ A cavalcade of anger and fear
- ☐ The rising winds of…
- ☐ She was cursed with a long and thin probing nose.
- ☐ The new guy continued to be bedeviled.
- ☐ Gratuitous use of bleeding edge technology
- ☐ My replacement was younger and more virile.
- ☐ It was a cloudy and tempestuous time.
- ☐ Flat field sunny day
- ☐ Wrong-headed ideas
- ☐ That was a dark period in our nation's history.
- ☐ Billy Goats Gruff
- ☐ The aura of moral crusade
- ☐ Drink from the unfiltered firehose of unvetted facts.
- ☐ Women swooned, or at least pretended to swoon.
- ☐ There's an empty cot in the bunkhouse tonight.
- ☐ Thrice-divorced
- ☐ Attractive simplicity
- ☐ Anoint
- ☐ I'm trying to be delicate here.
- ☐ The maiden with the flaxen hair
- ☐ Unusual experiences
- ☐ Quickly worsening attitude
- ☐ The chitter of insects
- ☐ Rare moment of clarity
- ☐ Genteel show of elegance
- ☐ Let me put this as delicately as possible.
- ☐ The youthful years of retirement

- ☐ That's a jaundiced way of looking at things.
- ☐ Emotionally scarring
- ☐ The clack of a skateboard
- ☐ Front and foremost
- ☐ He spoke with the quiver of a recently-spanked child.
- ☐ A different cup of fish
- ☐ Clutches of mothers
- ☐ Nipple-puckering cold
- ☐ Fetching to the eye
- ☐ Shield somebody's right
- ☐ A voice that could melt snow
- ☐ Assembly of the astute
- ☐ Victory has a hundred fathers but defeat is an orphan.
- ☐ Metaphors we live by
- ☐ The conveyor belt of evolution
- ☐ The foul breath of prostitutes
- ☐ Choppy waters
- ☐ Pure and radiant of heart
- ☐ A fern-filled room
- ☐ The president didn't have the power to muzzle the press.
- ☐ Not to put too fine of a point on it, but...
- ☐ The lilt of Irish laughter
- ☐ A fossilized marriage
- ☐ A wrinkle in time
- ☐ Political correctness contrasting common sense
- ☐ Contagious distempers
- ☐ Patrick is the answer to every maiden's prayer.
- ☐ They came in over the transom.
- ☐ A healthy life full of bounty
- ☐ A Taster's Choice moment
- ☐ Moistened with the watering can of evolutionary dew

TRYING TO WRITE THAT COLLEGE ENTRANCE EXAM? OR YOUR NEXT NOVEL? PONDERING JUST THE RIGHT WORDS TO BACKFILL THAT "HAPPY BIRTHDAY" CARD? INCORPORATE SOME OF THESE PHRASES INTO YOUR NEXT LITERARY EFFORT.

- ☐ Drumbeat of support
- ☐ Black hole of Calcutta
- ☐ Your fears have been proven unfounded.
- ☐ Benevolent arm twisting
- ☐ The static obscures the message.
- ☐ Yawning abyss
- ☐ Though talk has turned into a goo most foul...
- ☐ We are refreshed and challenged by your unique point of view.
- ☐ Furls of knowledge are laid at your feet.
- ☐ As a layman, I can appreciate your ignorance.
- ☐ Tangerine trees and marmalade skies
- ☐ In closing...
- ☐ I would crawl on glass to...
- ☐ A fainting attempt
- ☐ Deathly pallor
- ☐ To persevere in spite of damming criticism
- ☐ The local weatherman had a kinky mess of thinning blond hair that spiked up in unruly patches like crab grass.
- ☐ Inky shadows
- ☐ You shall see the face of God.
- ☐ X should not be sacrificed on the altar of Y.
- ☐ Just to camp on what Bill said...
- ☐ A sack-like chin
- ☐ Our swords have crossed.
- ☐ Faceless cavalcade
- ☐ Conspicuous consumption
- ☐ The evidence was circumstantial but persuasive.
- ☐ A new knife in the back of...
- ☐ The new guy was received with well-justified suspicion.
- ☐ Those men are made of stonier soil.
- ☐ Vastly inferior
- ☐ Serious misgivings

- ☐ Freshly swept rooms
- ☐ Wild intoxication of pride and joy
- ☐ A waterfall of creative alternatives
- ☐ Coldwater flat
- ☐ Deep lessons
- ☐ Knee-slapping, pee-in-your-pants good time
- ☐ Achingly beautiful
- ☐ Cadaverous frame
- ☐ Four cheese pizza, providing a plethora of cheese festival in your mouth.
- ☐ Telling stories irrespective of you audience's interest
- ☐ Load-bearing significance in the eco system
- ☐ Capacity and power
- ☐ Dipping your beak into the public trough
- ☐ Death traps of typhus, tuberculosis, hunger, and fire
- ☐ I ponder for accuracy, not for embarrassment.
- ☐ She was left laying on the shores of corporate headquarters, flopping and gasping for air.
- ☐ Your indignity has no resonance with me, so save it.
- ☐ Let me introduce Bill, from parts unknown.
- ☐ The seeds of meanness were blossoming.
- ☐ His actions are a finger in the eye of decency.
- ☐ Slack-jawed amazement
- ☐ You can smell the cogitation.
- ☐ Women of childbearing age have vanished from the face of the prairie as dramatically the buffalo.
- ☐ The blossom is off the rose.
- ☐ Institutional cover-ups preceding the accident
- ☐ That cost me deep in the purse.
- ☐ A Noahtain flood
- ☐ Little ripples versus big splashes
- ☐ The Fred Astaire dance poem
- ☐ The garbage was alive with rats.

- ☐ That would 'splain everything, Lucy.
- ☐ Verbal joust
- ☐ Escape the gravitational pull of...
- ☐ He laid down on the barbed wire of political correctness.
- ☐ Hardscrabble versus hard scrabble
- ☐ Hunting togs
- ☐ Charmingly draped in ivy
- ☐ Reproachful ghost
- ☐ Make no mistake about it.
- ☐ An untenable position
- ☐ Look the beast in the face.
- ☐ This is a three-pipe problem.
- ☐ Noble struggle
- ☐ The corridors of corporate America
- ☐ Contagious mirth
- ☐ A Mona Lisa smile
- ☐ Bastions of morality
- ☐ The memory still hurts and it still bleeds.
- ☐ With manic energy
- ☐ The project ran into some headwinds.
- ☐ Find that which otherwise men have missed.
- ☐ A fog-gauzed dream
- ☐ Broadly speaking
- ☐ Fall fast in the arms of Morpheus
- ☐ Let me tell you a story...
- ☐ Amber teeth and nicotine-stained fingernails
- ☐ When you're a Jet, you're a Jet all the way, from your first cigarette to your last dying day.
- ☐ Earl's speech was rich with metaphors and arid humor.
- ☐ Buffet of truth
- ☐ Elegantly dilapidated
- ☐ Personal slothfulness is the doorway to cowardice and cruelty.

- ☐ The cigar bar was thick with clouds of testosterone.
- ☐ A kind touch
- ☐ Evolution has progressed with exquisite slowness
- ☐ Elephants, boats and kiddie cars too. NOT elephant boats. Uncle Boogs was very particular about the way we sang that song.
- ☐ Fertile imagination

8. Occupations

Here are some of Uncle Boog's ideas about working for a living:

- "I lost my job as a psychic. I didn't see it coming."
- "Although hard work pays off in the future, laziness pays off now."

I don't think he would have made a very good career counselor.

- ☐ A hearing aid-wearing piano tuner
- ☐ Technology evangelist
- ☐ Wine seller
- ☐ Free soiler
- ☐ A knowledge worker
- ☐ Inept greenhorn
- ☐ A swamper
- ☐ Martial artist
- ☐ Fringe dweller
- ☐ Corn digger
- ☐ Geezer
- ☐ Amateur drycleaner
- ☐ An aging sports caster
- ☐ Beatnik
- ☐ A freelance social worker
- ☐ A bomb-throwing radical
- ☐ Streetwalker

ARE YOU TORMENTED BY THE QUESTION, "WHAT DO YOU WANT TO DO WHEN YOU GROW UP?"

USE THESE CHECK BOXES TO IDENTIFY SOME CAREERS WORTHY OF FURTHER RESEARCH.

- ☐ Poster boy for free speech
- ☐ Jerkline skinner
- ☐ Texas playboys from the Lone Star State
- ☐ A flight attendant on a cargo plane
- ☐ An easy job? Coroner—surgery on a dead person, and the worse that could happen is that you could get a pulse.
- ☐ A bureaucrat who swims in paper
- ☐ Dutch uncle
- ☐ Cow puncher
- ☐ Morale officer
- ☐ Edutrainer
- ☐ A spear catcher
- ☐ A professional moron
- ☐ The distinguished Senator from Hooterville
- ☐ Glum professor
- ☐ A flim flammer
- ☐ Stand up philosopher
- ☐ I have a job where I shower after work and not before work.
- ☐ Comedy juggernaut
- ☐ Opium smoker
- ☐ Hindenburg ground crew
- ☐ Tap dancer
- ☐ Body Nazis
- ☐ It is the trade of lawyers to question everything, yield nothing, and to talk by the hour.
- ☐ Beer squitter
- ☐ Bagman (an agent who collects proceeds of illicit activities)
- ☐ Limerist
- ☐ America's most outspoken dirt biker
- ☐ A gruntled employee
- ☐ Clown
- ☐ Portly provocateur

- ☐ A back slider
- ☐ Crackpot
- ☐ Cubical dweller
- ☐ Bastards in white lab coats who do experiments with goats
- ☐ A career that involves a bucket with wheels
- ☐ Army Rangers
- ☐ Tireless advocate for the poor
- ☐ Gay blade (a dashing swordsman)
- ☐ Chainsaw consultant
- ☐ Lint eater
- ☐ An aborigine who speaks in clicks
- ☐ Metaphysician
- ☐ Academic interloper
- ☐ Oysterman
- ☐ Bank guard in Anchorage Alaska, where everybody is wearing a ski mask
- ☐ Green Beret
- ☐ A teenage hacker with a curser in his left eye
- ☐ Bobsled designer
- ☐ Master Thespian
- ☐ Bubble dancer
- ☐ Alchemy major
- ☐ Platocrat
- ☐ Black Panther
- ☐ Submariner
- ☐ Picker
- ☐ A born-again Agnostic
- ☐ A sharecropper's son
- ☐ A one mule farmer
- ☐ Czar
- ☐ Second fiddle
- ☐ CaSHIER´ (an upscale cashier)
- ☐ Dithering ninny

- ☐ A confidence man, confidence trickster, conman
- ☐ Senior scientist at the Caltech Jet Propulsion Lab
- ☐ Apple knocker
- ☐ Zen Master
- ☐ Country bumpkin
- ☐ Rumor Control Officer
- ☐ Hyperbolist
- ☐ Hatemonger
- ☐ Cloistered academic working in the joy of pure science
- ☐ Beet Red Communist
- ☐ Devil chaser
- ☐ I've applied for a job: Acid Rescue.
- ☐ Seadog
- ☐ Pearl diver
- ☐ Alchemist
- ☐ Fixer
- ☐ Snake charmer
- ☐ Political pundit
- ☐ Professional turd
- ☐ A conjurer
- ☐ Devil's advocate
- ☐ News junkie

9. Senseless Acts of Violence

Don't get me wrong, Uncle Boogs wasn't normally a violent man. But we enjoyed many a good gangster movie and boxing match from his den.

Warning: *If you are faint of heart or have Violence Aversion Syndrome, be advised that this chapter may cause anguish. Consider skipping this chapter. You have been warned.*

- ☐ Break your spine
- ☐ Sit on a tack
- ☐ Thirty days in the electric chair
- ☐ Run roughshod
- ☐ Bite your head off and spit it down your throat
- ☐ Carl got wacked in the back of the head when he turned his back to the tetherball pole.
- ☐ Die of dysentery
- ☐ A political street fight
- ☐ Vent your spleen
- ☐ Beat him to death with a shovel
- ☐ High-risk behavior
- ☐ Beat him like a red-headed stepchild
- ☐ Go quail hunting with a howitzer
- ☐ I hate cancer. If cancer was a person, I would slap it.
- ☐ You wipe that smile off your face or I'll wipe it off for you.
- ☐ Never hit a man with glasses. Use a baseball bat.
- ☐ Death by a thousand cuts
- ☐ Get hit in the head with a Harley chain

- ☐ Take the pillow off the face of small business
- ☐ You'll be a splatter painting.
- ☐ Hit yourself in the head with a mallet.
- ☐ Fighting with a broken bourbon bottle
- ☐ A punch in the snoot
- ☐ OJ would like to knock the chip off Marsha Clark's shoulder with a sand wedge.
- ☐ You'll smoke a turd in hell for that.
- ☐ I'll rip your arm out of the socket and beat you with it.
- ☐ I've come here to chew bubble gum and kick some ass, and I'm all out of bubble gum.
- ☐ We were bombing the bunkers in Daiquiri.
- ☐ A poke in the eye of the American people
- ☐ Let's set some dumpsters on fire.
- ☐ Go postal
- ☐ Death by belt sander
- ☐ Drink hemlock
- ☐ So good it makes you want to slap your momma
- ☐ Jab your thumbs in the eyes of so-and-so
- ☐ Throw her under the bus
- ☐ The elephant is down and the tigers are circling.
- ☐ Verbally molest
- ☐ Kick your ass so hard you will wear it for a hat.
- ☐ Vaccinated with a phonograph needle
- ☐ Fighting the good fight
- ☐ You're foaming at the mouth.
- ☐ Lamb basting
- ☐ Steel cage death match
- ☐ Kick open the door.
- ☐ A picture of Norman Rockwell spanking a child
- ☐ He delivers babies using the Heimlich maneuver.
- ☐ The art of intimidation

- ☐ He was the kind of guy who liked pouring jet fuel on the camp fire.
- ☐ Throw rice at a wedding…real hard
- ☐ I'd sooner poke my eyes out with a hat pin.
- ☐ Vito's going to cut your tongue out and use it as a necktie.
- ☐ Bloody route
- ☐ Toss your cookies
- ☐ I just got throwed off the carousel of life.
- ☐ Once I lost a tooth playing football. My buddy found it several plays later and gave it to the coach. He threw it twenty yards and it was lost forever.
- ☐ A cat will almost always blink when hit by a hammer.
- ☐ Bring a tire tool to the piñata
- ☐ Admonish
- ☐ Back in the war, the Japs would charge us straightaway.
- ☐ If Michael Jackson went to prison, the inmates would pass him around like a joint.
- ☐ Give him the scolding of his life
- ☐ I'll throw you into another ZIP code.
- ☐ It was smashed to atoms.
- ☐ Street fighting: a good way to get your kicticals tested.
- ☐ Gag me with a spoon. Or fork.
- ☐ Rearrange your face
- ☐ Light the nuclear wick
- ☐ Kick some bunny
- ☐ Asthma attack: Two asthmatics jumped me behind the bowling alley. I should have heard them coming.
- ☐ Hold his head under water till the bubbles stop coming up.
- ☐ Unsuccessfully scaling the electric fence down by the rail yard
- ☐ Reckless, wholesale poisoning of people
- ☐ Fill my head with cannon balls and power my behind!
- ☐ Air-condition your skull

- ☐ Bare knuckle boxing
- ☐ The guy went postal!
- ☐ Naked rock fight
- ☐ If you aren't careful, Vito will move your face around.
- ☐ Walking on fire
- ☐ Never steal anything from anyone you can't outrun.
- ☐ Hurl some acid at...
- ☐ He was found face down in the Kool-Aid.
- ☐ I've never killed anybody with a hammer yet.
- ☐ Spaz attack
- ☐ A kick in the shorts
- ☐ Eye-gouging, ear-biting brawls
- ☐ Kick a hornet's nest
- ☐ The flowers she laid on her mother's grave were stolen from other gravesites.
- ☐ An ice pick to the eye
- ☐ Break some dishes
- ☐ Demonizing some and lionizing others
- ☐ We had to eat cat food all week, and when that ran out we ate the cat.
- ☐ I decided to go old school on him.
- ☐ Rib cracking
- ☐ Stick your head in a lion's mouth
- ☐ I served my apprenticeship with the rubber hose gang.
- ☐ When the ship hits the sand
- ☐ Leap off the cliff of euphoria and crash upon the rocks of remorse.
- ☐ Two harpoons already in her and she keeps swimming
- ☐ Don't break someone's heart, they have only one. Break their bones, they have 206 of them.
- ☐ His head was beaten to jelly by an iron pipe.
- ☐ I don't want to bring a boxer to a knife fight.
- ☐ The protester yelled her spittle-flinging disapproval.

- ☐ Kick stumps
- ☐ Have a rocket come out of your navel.
- ☐ I worked in a real pressure cooker.
- ☐ Fight the good fight
- ☐ Slap the taste out of your mouth
- ☐ Stomp one's ass
- ☐ Let's play Christians and lions.
- ☐ Beat him like a rented mule
- ☐ Tarred with the same brush
- ☐ Form a scrum
- ☐ Knock the fight out of the man
- ☐ Fired two warning shots...through the head
- ☐ Jerk my chain
- ☐ Mess with me, and I'll stick my foot so far up your ass, I'll lose my shoe.
- ☐ You can have my ribeye when you pry it from my cold, dead hands.
- ☐ Kick you in the juicebox
- ☐ The deadliest catch
- ☐ Dope slap
- ☐ In your face!
- ☐ I felt like sinking a meat hook into the boy's head and dragging him face down along the street while brandishing blunt scissors.
- ☐ A poke in the eye with a sharp shtick
- ☐ While you're honking, I'm reloading.
- ☐ Launch a salvo
- ☐ Tearing the head off the Ken doll
- ☐ The prisoner shoved the prison-issued sock down his throat and he gagged to death.
- ☐ So-and-so went ballistic
- ☐ Ouch! That's going to leave a mark.
- ☐ Beat the death out of you

- ☐ Before you can stab a rooster with a rusty screwdriver
- ☐ Drag everyone to their knees
- ☐ Be sent to your room without supper and get smothered
- ☐ We crossed swords.
- ☐ I'll give you something to cry about.
- ☐ A misunderstanding settled with crowbars
- ☐ Spill acid on someone
- ☐ Pass you around the prison like a peace pipe
- ☐ You really kicked some monk ass back there.
- ☐ An old-fashioned beating
- ☐ Eat shit and die.
- ☐ I'm working on a book urging the beating to death of baby whales using the bodies of baby seals.
- ☐ From a dark alley, whack a tourist up alongside the head with a two-by-four.
- ☐ Any time four New Yorkers get into a cab together without arguing, a bank robbery has just taken place.
- ☐ We're punching above our weight.

10. Spending Idle Time

Now I suppose, back in the day, when Uncle Boogs was growing up, people had to get creative passing the time. One day when he was a little bored, he sent a text to a random number saying "I hid the body…now what?" Listed below are some other alternatives for a rainy day.

- ☐ Play charades.
- ☐ Attend the daily crisis meeting.
- ☐ Use your ebbing strength to open the peanut butter jar.
- ☐ Suck a lemon dry.
- ☐ Throw off the heat-seeking missiles.
- ☐ Hang around taverns and fleshpots.
- ☐ Learn how to avoid rip-offs. Send $5 to the classified add titled *How to Avoid Rip-offs.*
- ☐ Debase your brain.
- ☐ Grow warts.
- ☐ Walk on the wild side.
- ☐ Jump in feet-first.
- ☐ Rain on the parade.
- ☐ Pussyfoot around.
- ☐ Marginalize someone.
- ☐ Go to Illinois and look for out-of-state license plates.
- ☐ Go shuck oysters.
- ☐ Pick up girls with your dad's Lincoln Mark IV.
- ☐ Think a long thought.
- ☐ Stump the band.

- ☐ Harbor animosity.
- ☐ Get pulled over for having too much blood in your alcohol.
- ☐ Step on your own air hose.
- ☐ Jerk your bobber.
- ☐ Replace pepper spray with silly string.
- ☐ Stand up, sit down, fight, fight, fight!
- ☐ Visit historic Frog Toe, Missouri.
- ☐ Assemble the SWAT team.
- ☐ Conduct an underwear check.
- ☐ Wait until hell freezes over and sit on the ice for a while.
- ☐ Poke it with a fork to see if it's done.
- ☐ Scrub it down.
- ☐ Freak out.
- ☐ Get loaded.
- ☐ Double the value of your pickup truck by adding a cell phone.
- ☐ Put a strobe light on cars instead of headlights, so other cars move in slow motion.
- ☐ Touch the third rail, I dare you.
- ☐ Hit the panic button.
- ☐ Follow the sun.
- ☐ Drive me out to the country on an old, deserted road, force me out of the car in front of the headlights, and make me dance the Carioca.
- ☐ Creep like a nun.
- ☐ Study the great books.
- ☐ Roll one for me.
- ☐ Tread carefully among the minefield of corporate politics.
- ☐ Keep a jaundiced eye on the man.
- ☐ Study the entrails of sacrificial lambs.
- ☐ Win friends and influence people.
- ☐ Worship the quicksand I walk on.
- ☐ Drink driving.

- ☐ Make chicken salad out of chicken shit.
- ☐ Scour the woods.
- ☐ Do some clowning.
- ☐ Sit on the couch and eat Yoplaits waiting for the Gilmore Girls to come on.
- ☐ Fight fifty brush fires at the same time.
- ☐ Get used to stale bread.
- ☐ Angle for the elusive sunfish.
- ☐ Watch the leaves fall from the trees.
- ☐ Rise out of the ashes like a Phoenix.
- ☐ Fix me a pitcher of your famous Mad Dog Margaritas.
- ☐ Clear the minefield.
- ☐ Live in domed cities with flying cars.
- ☐ Take away sharp objects and shoe laces.
- ☐ Use an acetylene torch.
- ☐ Sniff around a little bit.
- ☐ Go STRAIGHT to hell, and don't even stop at Jack-in-the-Box on the way.
- ☐ Eat your own dog food or drink your own Champagne.
- ☐ Pump out the bilge.
- ☐ Try to make water run uphill.
- ☐ Splash water on me to keep me from drying out.
- ☐ Tee yourself up for success.
- ☐ Learn how to carry water and chop wood.
- ☐ Trash talk.
- ☐ Rattle a cardboard saber.
- ☐ Put the genie back in the bottle.
- ☐ Host a clambake.
- ☐ Spin straw into straw.
- ☐ Cowboy up.
- ☐ Play him like a violin.
- ☐ Pick up your free postcard and wall calendar.
- ☐ Sit cross-legged on a mat.

☐ Militarize that.

☐ Re-circle the bullet holes.

☐ Start to randomly manipulate variables.

☐ Drive off your buzz.

☐ Get a hernia from coughing too hard.

☐ Attend a 1,000-women luncheon.

☐ Gloss over something at 20,000 feet.

☐ Pump the brakes.

☐ Find something broken and fix it.

☐ Massage your ego.

☐ Put the money on the stump and run.

☐ Throw for a loss.

☐ Noodling.

☐ Practice random acts of intelligence and senseless acts of self-control.

☐ Laugh and scratch.

☐ Max it out.

☐ Weep openly.

☐ Get "gooned" on vodka.

☐ Nip it in the bud.

☐ Navigate the rocky shoals.

☐ Donate two dollars to the inner-city headache fund.

PLANNING YOUR WEEKEND, VACATION, OR RETIREMENT? THIS CHAPTER OFFERS CREATIVE OPTIONS TO HELP YOU MAKE "GOOD DECISIONS." CHECK OFF A FEW YOU WANT TO FOLLOW UP ON.

☐ Fish in troubled waters.

☐ Go ahead, have TWO bowls of Frankenberry.

☐ Key in your VISA number.

☐ Pick up beer cans the morning after a party, recalling memories with each one.

☐ Take an acid trip.

☐ "Don't go home to your spouse this drunk, drive around a while."

☐ March with "Baby J."

☐ Put that doll away (quit talking about prior hurts).

- ☐ Walk twelve miles to school, uphill both ways.
- ☐ Be nice till it hurts.
- ☐ Cruise with the radio on.
- ☐ Go to Nordstrom Rack to pick up some "pieces."
- ☐ Use Goldfish snacks as coins.
- ☐ Go into the sea.
- ☐ Spread smallpox with wicked carelessness.
- ☐ Share a Coke at the Woolworth's lunch counter.
- ☐ Kanoodle.
- ☐ Wear the hair shirt of...
- ☐ Foment a rebellion.
- ☐ Steal cheese from Mighty Mouse.
- ☐ Spend time in a hammock with a parrot.
- ☐ Wake up and smell the sushi and sauerkraut.
- ☐ Pick lint from your blazer with tweezers.
- ☐ Throw the baby out with the bathwater.
- ☐ Promote the banjo as a musical instrument.
- ☐ Invest in Sizzler or Fotomat or Blockbuster.
- ☐ Donate your body to science fiction.
- ☐ Dominate airspace.
- ☐ Participate in naked, drunken luge, mixed doubles.
- ☐ Take the A-Train.
- ☐ Breed a scab on your nose.
- ☐ Sit on the rocky coast of Maine where old men mend fishing nets in the noonday sun.
- ☐ Hum *Nearer My God to Thee.*
- ☐ Play Blind Man's Bluff.
- ☐ Grow some stones.
- ☐ Do honorable work.
- ☐ Chew on something.
- ☐ Do a little snooping.
- ☐ Attend a special type of summer camp where arts and crafts include rolling cigarettes.

- ☐ Marinate yourself against anger and bitterness.
- ☐ Shake a stick at…
- ☐ Walk and talk in good cheer.
- ☐ Gripe your cookies.
- ☐ Saunter through the bar to find your favorite stool.
- ☐ Thread a needle.
- ☐ Go off on a tangerine.
- ☐ Soothe my brow with a damp compress.
- ☐ Run to the end of your chain and bark.
- ☐ Scream like a banshee.
- ☐ Attend group therapy by yourself
- ☐ Tap the brakes.
- ☐ Volunteer for a colonoscopy.
- ☐ Call the bomb squad, we're having a blast.
- ☐ Put your thinking cap on.
- ☐ Watch the *Hee Haw* channel for 24 hours.
- ☐ Play gin rummy for match sticks.
- ☐ Set the way-back machine, Sherman!
- ☐ Run with the fittest.
- ☐ Assume room temperature.
- ☐ Date the Doublemint Twins.
- ☐ Play that funky music.
- ☐ Be creative and make a new mistake.
- ☐ Hang around with strumpets and petty thieves.
- ☐ Go suck on your own tongue.
- ☐ Boil down the cabbage.
- ☐ Do a mating dance.
- ☐ Push the envelope.
- ☐ Look busy, Jesus is coming.
- ☐ Shoot from the lip.
- ☐ Lose your mind by drinking shoe polish.
- ☐ Organize your spice rack.
- ☐ Change the flavor of Coke again.

- ☐ Play Touch-and-Feel.
- ☐ Call me old-fashioned.
- ☐ Play Frisbee with a beer keg.
- ☐ Insert yourself.
- ☐ Rotate your tires.
- ☐ Put the key in the lock and turn it.
- ☐ Check your lug nuts.
- ☐ Secure the hatch and pressurize the cabin.
- ☐ Light the rocket and let me go.
- ☐ Scratch me where I itch.
- ☐ Live under a rock.
- ☐ Start your angina.
- ☐ Drink your weight in wolf poison.
- ☐ Give me the stink eye.
- ☐ Stay in character.
- ☐ Study cooperage at a distillery.
- ☐ Bob for French fries.
- ☐ Call the National Guard, we're having a riot!
- ☐ Do spadework.
- ☐ Attend a party where everyone lights their hair on fire.
- ☐ Go to the combine races.
- ☐ Whet your appetite.
- ☐ Amass appropriate help granules.
- ☐ Get on the horn.
- ☐ Play in the dirt with little scraps of wood.
- ☐ Attend the 100-mechanics march.
- ☐ Get a little shut-eye.
- ☐ Pull the queen of spades out of somebody's ear.
- ☐ Go out on the town and do some boot scooting in the local honky-tonk while your husband lays at home, dying by the inch.
- ☐ Ride the gravy train.
- ☐ Start gathering string on that topic.

- ☐ Hit those chips with another dash of salsa.
- ☐ Go to the liquor store to buy a case of impaired judgment.
- ☐ Visualize whirled peas.
- ☐ Play cards with two retired knee breakers.
- ☐ Suck on a washrag.
- ☐ Drive on a parkway and park on a driveway.
- ☐ Skate on the other side of the ice.
- ☐ Draw a chalk outline around Steve.
- ☐ Keep your shirt on.
- ☐ Wear platform shoes to a Kiss concert.
- ☐ Flirt with disaster.
- ☐ Send in the clowns.
- ☐ Get my goat.
- ☐ Spend an afternoon in hell.
- ☐ Call me on your princess phone.
- ☐ Allow silence to accumulate.
- ☐ Install firewalls.
- ☐ Exchange gases with the atmosphere.
- ☐ Cajole.
- ☐ Put a hose in your tailpipe.
- ☐ Share a box of wine.
- ☐ Put some slide in your stride and pep in your step.
- ☐ Take it to a higher order.
- ☐ Hide from exercise with the Fitness Protection Program.
- ☐ Distill information.
- ☐ Look at bark pattern.
- ☐ Visit the Congo during scorpion season.
- ☐ Lock down the landing gear.
- ☐ Fold, spindle, and mutilate.
- ☐ Trash your mind.
- ☐ Ramble on.
- ☐ Drop him like a hot crack pipe.
- ☐ Master basic skills.

- ☐ Ride the elephant.
- ☐ Stand there and yell at the moon.
- ☐ Play freeze tag.
- ☐ Snag a morsel of cat food.
- ☐ Watch Scotty grow.
- ☐ Establish foot holds.
- ☐ Shake a leg.
- ☐ Drain the brain juices.
- ☐ Watch TV in your underwear with a beer.
- ☐ Shit eggrolls.
- ☐ Wrap your hands around a gyro while visiting Greece.
- ☐ Put a lock on it.
- ☐ Smuggle the baby Dalai Lama out of Tibet.
- ☐ Talk eye-to-eye with an optometrist.
- ☐ Preach paupership.
- ☐ Live in a just and verdant world.
- ☐ Mouse around.
- ☐ Stay at a motel where you are sure that there were enough lamp shades to go around.
- ☐ Cogitate.
- ☐ Simonize our watches.
- ☐ Idle vaporing.
- ☐ Light the fuse.
- ☐ Make buggy whips.
- ☐ Lower the boom.
- ☐ Fall into habits of inebriation and folly.
- ☐ Wash up on the beach.
- ☐ Connect the dots.
- ☐ Level the cinderblocks under your house.
- ☐ Engage in name calling.
- ☐ File off serial numbers.
- ☐ Go around the corner on two wheels.
- ☐ Penetrate the jamming signal.

- ☐ Slide down the razor blade of life.
- ☐ Fan dance.
- ☐ Go suck eggs.
- ☐ Feather your nest.
- ☐ Go clod hoppin'.
- ☐ Load the dice.
- ☐ Eat your lunch at your desk out of a complex system of Tupperware.
- ☐ Live in a no-fly zone.
- ☐ Smoke a joint the size of a thumb.
- ☐ Paint passing lines on curved roads.
- ☐ Worship at the altar of…
- ☐ Stutter in Spanish.
- ☐ Message the data.
- ☐ Sharpen the saw.
- ☐ Let bathwater stand in the tub for a week and sell it as a green throw rug.
- ☐ Fester world problems.
- ☐ Pop your cork.
- ☐ Shoot from half court and score.
- ☐ Go to the store and watch them change fruit.
- ☐ Fry bigger fish.
- ☐ Attend scrum meetings.
- ☐ Go to a happy place.
- ☐ Put that in your pipe and weld it.
- ☐ Take the sidewalks in at night.
- ☐ Stump the chump.
- ☐ Open the kimono.
- ☐ Fart fairy dust.
- ☐ Play in the street.
- ☐ Crystalize concepts.
- ☐ Read the prayer of the dead, and whoever cries the loudest gets the prize.

- Fold proteins.
- Swing the alphabet like the Three Stooges. (B-A-bay, B-E-be, B-I-bicky-bi, B-O-bow, Bicky-bi-bow-B-U-boo, etc.)
- Drink raspberry-lime rickeys while sunbathing on the sorority house roof.
- Touch the face of God.
- Inhale your own gas.
- Go sky larking.
- Chase after small animals with a weed eater.
- At a party with a bunch of guys, argue if it's possible to jump from a given balcony to a given roof or swimming pool.
- Rotate like a chunk of gyro meat to stay warm.
- Soil your soul.
- Knock on Formica.
- Be a caustic critic.
- Go to a BBQ where you're the only one with fingers.
- Get your panties in a bunch.
- Dress up like a referee and go to Footlocker.
- Forage for food.
- Read the riot act.
- Sing Hosannas to…
- Lick the bowl? You'll have to hold me upside down in the toilet.
- Fill your goblet of happiness.
- Engage in mental gymnastics.
- Feed the bulldog.
- Fall between the cracks.
- Study the Battle of Hastings.
- Take him down for questioning.
- Talk in whale talk.
- Play naked twister.
- Pray for clement weather.

- ☐ Draw a red herring across the trail.
- ☐ Go to a store, buy some ammo, and ask if they also sell ski masks.
- ☐ Go fox tossing.
- ☐ Play crack the whip.
- ☐ Brain surgery without anesthesia.
- ☐ Spit wooden golf balls.
- ☐ Swallow the bitter pill.
- ☐ Get down to the important business of cracking eggs.
- ☐ Put your nuzzles to the oars.
- ☐ Join a marching handbell choir.
- ☐ Break in a new pair of shoes.
- ☐ Debone the magazines (take out the ads and subscription cards prior to reading).
- ☐ Leave the reservation.
- ☐ Float an air biscuit.
- ☐ Mono-task.
- ☐ Take notes in your diary.
- ☐ Throw a towel on the razor wire and climb over it.
- ☐ Chew tobacco.
- ☐ Game the system.
- ☐ Roll up your sleeves and thread the profusion catheter.
- ☐ Major in dance history.
- ☐ Start a whiffle ball game.
- ☐ Shepherd.
- ☐ Open up a new can of Pringles.
- ☐ Shit the bed.
- ☐ Rattle around in your room.
- ☐ He's trying to get me into the tent and give me a sermon.
- ☐ Dive into the shallow end of the quarry pond.
- ☐ Chew on glass.
- ☐ Put a lid on it.
- ☐ Cobble something together.

- ☐ Flip your wig.
- ☐ Discuss with fat people how to sweat.
- ☐ Correlate, assimilate, and message information.
- ☐ Talk to a bar full of manic depressives two minutes after happy hour.
- ☐ Get caught in your own syrup.
- ☐ Spike the football.
- ☐ Try to scotch tape together the memories of what you did last night.
- ☐ Go bananas.
- ☐ Never overplay your hand.
- ☐ Organize an endless handwringing group.
- ☐ Untangle a conundrum.
- ☐ Suck the oxygen out of the air.
- ☐ Join the Grand Forks Pitch Fork Drill Team.
- ☐ Create glee among dotard people.

11. Proclamations

What's the difference between a proclamation from the Vatican and a mail-order husband from eBay? One's a Papal mandate and the other's a PayPal man-date.

So what follows aren't proclamations in the traditional sense, not like decrees. Instead, they're more like assertions, statements of fact and fiction—what Uncle Boogs used to say when he hit his thumb with a hammer, or when he was confronted by awkward silence.

- ☐ Sweet cheeses!
- ☐ Precisely the case.
- ☐ I don't know whether to kill myself or go bowling.
- ☐ I'd rather chew glass, the kind that gets stuck in your throat.
- ☐ I'm not nice, I'm just two-faced.
- ☐ Well, douche me with dishwater.
- ☐ Even cowgirls get the blues.
- ☐ Somewhere a village is missing its idiot.
- ☐ I live in a town famous for controversy.
- ☐ Instead of lubricating me, get to the truth.
- ☐ I need to buy a vowel.
- ☐ He can really pepper the gumbo.
- ☐ He had Doris Day for a parole officer.
- ☐ 'Spec the unexpected.
- ☐ I was stationed in Drambuie, North Africa.
- ☐ Pardon my hyperbole.

- ☐ I was as happy as a little girl.
- ☐ Don't look directly at Karen.
- ☐ Even Einstein is scared.
- ☐ Cough hard. Harder!
- ☐ I miss your face.
- ☐ Let's get this turkey in the oven.
- ☐ Never turn your back to the chief during the corn dance.
- ☐ I'll be a monkey's uncle!
- ☐ By the time I was three, I could resole a shoe.
- ☐ That's the last straw!
- ☐ That's the spirit!
- ☐ I was impressed with her womanly charms.
- ☐ That idea meets the giggle test.
- ☐ Once again, Bill raises an important point for us to consider.
- ☐ I smoke in moderation—only one cigar at a time.
- ☐ I was wearing a jacket like that the first time I got beat to hell.
- ☐ Holy crow!
- ☐ Roll Call: "Present, and honored to be so."
- ☐ In control and ready to go.
- ☐ I've lost the will to live
- ☐ Stick it up your nose.
- ☐ When your IQ gets to eight, sell.
- ☐ May a sick yak leave a deposit in your dune buggy.
- ☐ A lot of moving parts!
- ☐ I graduated Kumbaya.
- ☐ I'm a thick crust guy.
- ☐ When a pig becomes a hog, it's time for slaughter.
- ☐ I won't expose myself to that hazard.
- ☐ No disrespect intended.
- ☐ I confess, I took the Lindbergh baby.
- ☐ A cubicle is just a padded cell without a door.

- ☐ I was born modest, but not all over.
- ☐ That scrapes my whitewalls.
- ☐ We're not asking you to splice DNA.
- ☐ Hiking and alcohol don't mix.
- ☐ I've seen better heads on boils.
- ☐ This is Houston.
- ☐ World peace, is not a quick fix.
- ☐ Irony can be pretty ironic.
- ☐ Nobody should write their own autobiography till after they're dead.
- ☐ And his mother cried.
- ☐ I thought you were trying to hocus me.
- ☐ Ouch, is grossly inadequate!
- ☐ I work in a reality distortion field.
- ☐ You want green peppers? Come to my garden and I'll give you some green peppers!
- ☐ Look at me with your good eye.
- ☐ Well, dog my cats!
- ☐ I'm the one with egg on my face.
- ☐ Well cut off my legs and call me "Shorty"!
- ☐ I started out as a child.
- ☐ Be careful, you may get a nose bleed.
- ☐ Semper Fi.
- ☐ Fish or cut bait.
- ☐ Spoken like a true smartass.
- ☐ I'm not being hyperbolic.
- ☐ I've never stolen anything from anybody who didn't deserve it.
- ☐ I'd stab somebody in the neck with a fork.
- ☐ Round here, we do things a little differently.
- ☐ I'm just here to establish an alibi.
- ☐ I live in a post-truth environment.
- ☐ Ambivalent? Well, yes and no.

- ☐ The persecution rests.
- ☐ Horseradish!
- ☐ I'm a little jumpy.
- ☐ Weeping Jesus on the cross…
- ☐ Don't piss on my back and tell me it's raining!
- ☐ I would rather run through a junkyard in bare feet.
- ☐ Lay it on me.
- ☐ That's the jackpot question.
- ☐ Like hell.
- ☐ May you be sucked under in a vat of hot fudge.
- ☐ That would scare the horses.
- ☐ I'm up to my clavicle in…
- ☐ Don't give it a thought.
- ☐ Stick a fork in me, I'm done.
- ☐ Great day in the morning!
- ☐ Ed McMahon is here with a check.
- ☐ I've been smoking for thirty-five years and my lung feels great.
- ☐ Those aren't bed bugs, they're just regular bugs.
- ☐ I'd like to put it on a gift certificate.
- ☐ You all remember to wipe your feet.
- ☐ Shirley, you can't be serious!
- ☐ Jumping butterballs!
- ☐ I'm not superstitious, just a little stitious.
- ☐ My hands are tied.
- ☐ Selling like hotcakes.
- ☐ I'm seldom wrong in these matters.
- ☐ These tired old bones…
- ☐ I am being chased by Count Chocula!
- ☐ You underrate yourself.
- ☐ What in heaven's name?
- ☐ No guts, no gravy.

- ☐ Let there be dancing in the streets, drinking in the bars, and necking in the parlor.
- ☐ Your helmet is on too tight.
- ☐ If you fart in an echo chamber, you'll never hear the end of it.
- ☐ Big wheels keep on turning.
- ☐ It takes a big man to admit he's wrong. I'm not a big man.
- ☐ I'm such a bad gardener that I can't grow good weeds.
- ☐ Go, and God bless.
- ☐ Holly Golly!
- ☐ I wept openly.
- ☐ Save you some shoe leather…
- ☐ I'd rather cut into my skull with a bone saw and feel my own brains.
- ☐ I've been through many significant emotional situations. And some of them have actually happened.
- ☐ I was just screwing around in the woods; no women were involved.
- ☐ I belong to a bridge club. I jump next Tuesday.
- ☐ I used to sport apostolic hair.
- ☐ I know what I'm doing.
- ☐ Quick, before the sun sets.
- ☐ I'm not fat…I'm abundant.
- ☐ Holy Ned!
- ☐ Hot Dog!
- ☐ Shiver my timbers!
- ☐ Drat!
- ☐ He really knows his beans.
- ☐ "Hello, you're on *Car Talk*."
- ☐ Listen up. I've got nothing to say, so I'm only going to say it once.
- ☐ "Oh, bother," said Pooh as a sniper took out Piglet.

SOMETIMES "DARN IT" AND "OH WELL" JUST DON'T CUT IT. YOU CAN DO BETTER.

USE THE CHECKBOXES TO INCORPORATE FRESH PHRASES INTO YOUR NEW PARLANCE.

- ☐ There is no hope, but I may be wrong.
- ☐ "Contagious?" I asked the doctor. " 'REAL contagious,' " he tells me.
- ☐ Don't use the word *relationship* unless you really have to.
- ☐ Listen, "Rosemary"…
- ☐ It was a light-your-hair-on-fire good party.
- ☐ Pie crusts and promises are made to be broken.
- ☐ I've worn dresses with higher hemlines than your IQ.
- ☐ I haven't factored that into my statement.
- ☐ After eating lunch in the cafeteria, I've got enough gas to get to Pittsburgh.
- ☐ I'm not as think as you drunk I am.
- ☐ Never trust a puppet.
- ☐ Somebody has to carry the water.
- ☐ I spent my childhood in the bottom drawer.
- ☐ Dim the lights and raise the curtain.
- ☐ It's toast!
- ☐ I will never engage in a winter sport that has an ambulance parked at the bottom of the hill.
- ☐ You lucky man!
- ☐ Take the cake!
- ☐ I can smell fear.
- ☐ Over and out.
- ☐ Thank you, Mr. Peabody.
- ☐ I want to be buried in my Tina Turner dress.
- ☐ It's hard to water your fern in a room of screaming women.
- ☐ You bowled a lot of strikes, but you left one standing.
- ☐ The crucifix around his neck had a real live guy on it.
- ☐ Liar, liar, pants on fire!
- ☐ Fiddlesticks!
- ☐ So, I told the doctor, "That's it. As of this morning I quit my medication, homicidal tendencies be damned!"

☐ I grew up at a time that, if there were problems at school, it was probably my fault.

☐ I'm not your type. I'm not inflatable.

☐ I was hit by a piece of lighting.

☐ I'd rather cut off a finger with some pruning shears.

☐ My mouth was spitless.

☐ A little dab'll do ya.

☐ Cooler, man!

☐ Doing that would send a loud and unpleasant message.

☐ I'll have to stay off heavy machinery again today.

☐ Well bust my buttons, that's a horse of a different color!

☐ Rut ro, Reorge!

☐ I know Jack Shit.

☐ Long may your chimney smoke.

☐ My yellow light is flashing.

☐ May you share a bowl of poi with an unclean holy man.

☐ This property is governed by the castle doctrine.

☐ Honey, we don't put our fingers in our butt.

☐ I'm not the fastest wicket in the stick.

☐ Goll-dern it!

☐ Blackmail is a powerful tool.

☐ Everybody wants to eat off a clean plate but nobody wants to do the dishes.

☐ You are evil and must be destroyed.

☐ We will need a laser to cut that off.

☐ I swallowed the Blarney Stone.

☐ Somebody is going to need to lower their expectations.

☐ I just peed a little.

☐ It is illegal to offer a monkey a cigarette in the state of New Jersey.

☐ Easy. Piece of kelp.

☐ That son of a bitch even makes malts.

☐ Don't bother me. I'm living happily ever after.

- ☐ Oh, slush!
- ☐ Chaos, panic, and disorder—my work here is done.
- ☐ Tell me "yes" or "no" in five words or less.
- ☐ Spelling is a losd art.
- ☐ I feel your pain.
- ☐ I've got the yips.
- ☐ Holy fright!
- ☐ Most people miss the sophisticated point you make.
- ☐ What in the blazes?
- ☐ This is curtains!
- ☐ Off to the gallows!
- ☐ Silly old sausage.
- ☐ I have a carton of cigarettes that need smoking.
- ☐ My nipples are getting perky.
- ☐ It was running down both legs.
- ☐ Drink your orange juice and get out there.
- ☐ Silly buggers
- ☐ Why, when I was a young Jedi…
- ☐ It's a good day to whoop somebody's ass.
- ☐ Allergic to constructive criticism.
- ☐ I go where the puck should be.
- ☐ We go till they say no, then we fight them some more.
- ☐ Here are the keys to my dune buggy.
- ☐ I'm off like a prom dress.
- ☐ I drive an exotic car, a French Riviera.
- ☐ If I had my druthers…
- ☐ That grates my cheese!
- ☐ Let the horse run and let the rider ride.
- ☐ Well, tie my feet and call me doggie…
- ☐ Three bags full, yes sir.
- ☐ I often remember…
- ☐ I can't remember if I'm the good twin or the evil one…
- ☐ Even Stevie Wonder could see that bad call.

- ☐ I'd have a better chance of playing pick-up-sticks with my butt cheeks.
- ☐ That makes my skin tingle.
- ☐ Great Scott!
- ☐ I know what you're thinking, Dorothy.
- ☐ Hare Krishna!
- ☐ Christ on a bicycle!
- ☐ This kitten's got a whip!
- ☐ My brother from another mother!
- ☐ You're keeping me in suspenders!
- ☐ Next thing you know, old Jed's a millionaire.
- ☐ I've spent most of my money on beer and women...the rest I just wasted.
- ☐ Never trust a hooker with fresh breath.
- ☐ Norwegian's last words: "I'm just fine."
- ☐ This isn't an office. It's hell with fluorescent lighting.
- ☐ My word!
- ☐ At least if I'm sent to prison, the prison guard will discover my prostate cancer.
- ☐ Mind your own biscuits!
- ☐ There are no more favors left in the cookie jar.
- ☐ Don't look at me in that tone of voice!
- ☐ I'm comfortable with being out of control.
- ☐ You're not fat, you're just...easier to see.
- ☐ Don't bring me an old mangy dog and ask me to play like she's Lassie.
- ☐ Puns don't kill people, people kill people.
- ☐ My doctor put me on the patch.
- ☐ You're darn tootin'!
- ☐ It ain't the size that counts, well no...it is the size.
- ☐ One of us is thinking about sex...okay, it's me.
- ☐ I've been married seven times in five years. Wedding rehearsal? Hell I could be the instructor.

- ☐ They call me "Tater Salad."
- ☐ Have a Coke and a smile.
- ☐ Oh, that's too bad.
- ☐ Over the moon.
- ☐ It's bad luck to kill a dog with a cake knife.
- ☐ Okie Dokie!
- ☐ Yeah, that's the ticket!
- ☐ Go forth and multiply.
- ☐ That wound needs to be sutured.
- ☐ Oh, you slay me!
- ☐ I'm shooting Ektachrome.
- ☐ Marginal employees are always at their best.
- ☐ I've got to get my rest; tomorrow is Arbor Day.
- ☐ A lot of pain there.
- ☐ Sarcasm is just one more service we offer.
- ☐ I have no tested fighting skills.
- ☐ I do oppressions.
- ☐ A pox upon you!
- ☐ The joint is jumping.
- ☐ May your tribe increase.
- ☐ Nice chance, snowball.
- ☐ After a big meal, I can't button my cuffs.
- ☐ I think it's something we ought to do, and by *we,* I mean *you.*
- ☐ The *Titanic* sails at dawn.
- ☐ I slept the sleep of the dead.
- ☐ God bless the baby.
- ☐ I was driving down the highway when the prescription on my glasses ran out.
- ☐ You're going to be in real trouble, real fast.
- ☐ The economy was left in tatters.
- ☐ I've got these pain pills that makes childbirth a pleasure.
- ☐ I'm just a young kid with a dream.

- [ ] I'm not crazy, I've just been in a bad mood for forty years.
- [ ] Yes, I know the muffin man.
- [ ] Same wreck, different train.
- [ ] It is easier to wear slippers than to carpet the world.
- [ ] Trespassers will be shot. Survivors will be reshot.
- [ ] I was raised with *Hooked on Phonics.*
- [ ] "Jinx!" Or "Thank you, Mr. Jinx."
- [ ] I was retreaded.
- [ ] He thinks you're stupefying.
- [ ] I fart, just like everybody else.
- [ ] A girl's got to do what a girl's got to do.
- [ ] Do this expediently.
- [ ] Back me up on this.
- [ ] Today is Change the Damned Sheets day.
- [ ] I'm too close to the blast.
- [ ] Everything's unicorns and rainbows.
- [ ] No objections, your honor.
- [ ] Try it, you'll like it.
- [ ] It happened on my watch.
- [ ] I'm not in my second childhood. I never left my first.
- [ ] I love the smell of Glade Plugs-Ins in the morning.
- [ ] And it never leaves that nasty aftertaste in your mouth.
- [ ] If your watch is slow, two hours slow, move to California.
- [ ] Then came Bronson.
- [ ] She's one more hurt away from leaving you.
- [ ] Bring me a goblet of something cool and refreshing and a hog head on a platter, too.
- [ ] Join the military...they'll make you pull up your pants.
- [ ] Mom was never a biker chick, but some of her buddies claimed she resembled one.
- [ ] Well, I'll be dipped in gravy and rolled in cracker crumbs!
- [ ] I went to go blow up a bus but I burned my lips on the exhaust pipe.

- ☐ Be just and fear not.
- ☐ I was elected homecoming poet.
- ☐ May a weird holy man carry your mother off piece by piece.
- ☐ The mother of all...(fill in your own)
- ☐ There's a lot of hard work and heavy lifting ahead.
- ☐ Hello, Jenny Craig!
- ☐ Hit the road.
- ☐ I was voted class clown my student teaching year.
- ☐ Okay, boomer.
- ☐ I've never done that before, but I think I'd be damned good at it.
- ☐ Everything about him was superlative.
- ☐ I can't shake suckers out of my sleeve.
- ☐ Either get busy living or get busy dying.
- ☐ This is mission control.
- ☐ I've been married for thirty-five years and it's getting pretty serious.
- ☐ I feel a productive afternoon coming on. (after a big lunch)
- ☐ Goes without saying.
- ☐ I'd rather have a plane crash in the Andes and have to live off my fellow passengers.
- ☐ Even God is uneasy.
- ☐ Wheels up!
- ☐ Sarcasm is one of my many talents.
- ☐ Bless her little heart.
- ☐ It was damned scary.
- ☐ The headband of your hardhat is on too tightly.
- ☐ Fat old people go in the hospital and come out thin, old thin people go in the hospital and come out dead.
- ☐ Even Mark Spitz couldn't swim with that millstone around his neck.
- ☐ When monkeys jump out of my ass!

- ☐ That sport makes my liver curl.
- ☐ All the men in my family were bearded. And most of the women, too.
- ☐ Danger is my companion.
- ☐ It's not a political convention, it's a crime scene.
- ☐ If you say something real fast, it sounds easy.
- ☐ May I be struck with three bolts of lightning.
- ☐ Luck is with me.
- ☐ Hold your horses!
- ☐ Shoot low sheriff, I think she's riding a Shetland!
- ☐ Close your eyes before you bleed to death!
- ☐ We may be together in the same storm, but we are not in the same boat.
- ☐ Listen Chico—do you mind if I call you Chico?
- ☐ Bees knees!
- ☐ Just like that.
- ☐ Honey, I'd be happy to agree with you. But if I did, we'd BOTH be wrong.
- ☐ Don't dig up snakes in order to kill them.
- ☐ Nothing can go wrong now.
- ☐ This is my ninth stint in rehab.
- ☐ Now the shoe is on the other foot.
- ☐ I feel cleansed just talking with you.
- ☐ We didn't know if you were coming by land or sea.
- ☐ I heard that the terrorists attacked Croatia! Damn, I went to high school with her!
- ☐ I've seen chair legs with more ambition than that.
- ☐ I majored in patricide.
- ☐ Why, thank you. Please remain seated.
- ☐ For inquiring minds like mine, yeah, I've got MENSA written all over me.
- ☐ I'm no psychologist, but I do own a couch.

- ☐ If at first you don't succeed, give up and don't make an ass of yourself.
- ☐ Write this down, Einstein.
- ☐ May the fleas of a thousand camels invade your armpits.
- ☐ I'm praying to the Lord, and the devil on the side.
- ☐ Our motel room even had wall-to-wall carpet!
- ☐ We're here for fun and it's all for charity!
- ☐ It isn't the heat, it's the stupidity.
- ☐ Open Sesame!
- ☐ Don't trust him, and don't let him pick up soap at the YMCA.
- ☐ Leapin' lizards!
- ☐ His last words…"Life's a bitch."
- ☐ Fine and dandy.
- ☐ Don't make me laugh, I may wet my pants!
- ☐ It only rains on me.
- ☐ The world is flat.
- ☐ Procrastination…do it today.
- ☐ Get ready on the kill switch!
- ☐ My doctor is the best ear, nose, and wallet guy out there.
- ☐ Well saw off my leg and call me shorty.
- ☐ My life is a toilet bowl of meaningless fluff.
- ☐ I'm not too long on brains.
- ☐ Don't worry, it's a dry heat.
- ☐ If my nose was full of nickels, I'd blow it all on you.
- ☐ Thanks for the news, Tom Brokaw.
- ☐ Please and thank you.
- ☐ For every broken heart on Broadway, there's also a broken window.
- ☐ Good golly!
- ☐ I am fifty-one linear years old.
- ☐ Good cooks never serve vegetables you can't spell.
- ☐ You need to drink a big glass of shut-the-hell-up!

- Surely!
- Nertz!
- I'll have to turn in my man-card.
- Nice try, Jacques Cousteau.
- You MUST try the decaf!
- They call me "Isotope Dave."
- This is way tangential.
- I gave up kiwi and mangos for Lent.
- I do not look becoming in my biking costume.
- Play it cool, Juul.
- I knocked on more doors than Mary and Joseph.
- But luck was with us!
- I know the ancient dances.
- I got a little steamed.
- She would not kiss his blood-caked lips.
- We're not shopping for tube socks here!
- Don't hit the wrong nail.
- Before you can say "Jack Robinson"!
- Friends don't let friends drive Yugos.
- My give-a-damn is busted.
- For crying out loud!
- Mom never had any idea of my lowly school status.
- I'm a deep-dish kind of guy.
- I'd rather sit on a flaming hibachi!
- He's new to the herd.
- Don't touch that sundial!
- Armageddon? Arma gettin' outta here!
- I'm a Gemini, and so am I.
- Don't get your panties in a wad.
- I'm not tense, just terribly, terribly alert.
- I do best following animal or child acts.
- B-minor, the saddest of all keys.
- You said a mouthful.

- ☐ I believe you may be a good candidate for membership in my club for mutual improvement.
- ☐ If "if's" and "but's" were candy and nuts, it would be a merry Christmas for all.
- ☐ Quit assing around.
- ☐ Suffering succotash!
- ☐ I'm taking the cork out of the bottle, so prepare yourself to take a whiff when I pass it around.
- ☐ I go to church every gosh-darn Sunday.
- ☐ I spend my spare time curling in the fetal position.
- ☐ My hands are clean.
- ☐ I'm no Albert Schweitzer.
- ☐ Never say never—oops, I just said it twice.
- ☐ I used to like tuna better, back when it had dolphin in it.
- ☐ When in doubt, spit it out!
- ☐ I never show my body to a man of the same gender.
- ☐ Can't win for losing!
- ☐ I don't work much. I'm a consultant.
- ☐ The weather started getting rough.
- ☐ Winner, winner, chicken dinner!
- ☐ I am a junior FBI agent.
- ☐ Take my advice: wear the underwear without the ketchup stains.
- ☐ Get it done before the second coming.
- ☐ I'm just a penny sitting on a wrong train track.
- ☐ Lean meat don't fry.
- ☐ Mind your own beeswax.
- ☐ I can suck beer through a layer of sheetrock.
- ☐ Shut the front door! (shut up)
- ☐ They called him "Salty Boogers."
- ☐ Name that tune in one note.
- ☐ I'm from the hair-splitting department.
- ☐ Be less acid.

- [ ] That comment chafed me.
- [ ] I can't lift weights. They're too heavy.
- [ ] You scared the fire out of me.
- [ ] The compass of Truth is spinning out of control.
- [ ] I got to go back home and tell Starsky.
- [ ] I can't drive an automatic
- [ ] I am Fetus, King of Placenta!
- [ ] Holy socks!
- [ ] I'm dedicated to saving the end zone layer.
- [ ] I'm no Dr. Fauci...
- [ ] I can't shoot rockets out of my ass. Anymore.
- [ ] Pay no attention to the man behind the curtain!
- [ ] The Trans Am was unable to successfully maneuver "Dead Man's Curve."
- [ ] My life is out of balance.
- [ ] Wait a minute, Chester...
- [ ] This will be our last transmission.
- [ ] I'd hate to be around when Mike hits the fan.
- [ ] Thank you, baby Jesus!
- [ ] Operators are standing by.
- [ ] My work here is done.
- [ ] One of you will be a prom queen.
- [ ] I'm sorry, you're only the fourth caller.
- [ ] I feel like I died and went to hell.
- [ ] Men ate what they had not raised.
- [ ] My jaw figuratively dropped off my face.
- [ ] Man down!
- [ ] I don't think so, Scooter!
- [ ] I'd throw myself down a flight of stairs for...
- [ ] I'm a large-boned guy and when I get up to offer a woman a seat, three get to sit down.
- [ ] Cerebrate good times, come on!
- [ ] You give me the creeps!

- ☐ You make me a little jumpy.
- ☐ Somebody needs to put out the dumpster fire.
- ☐ I was swiftboated.
- ☐ My life has been changed.
- ☐ Work is my middle name.
- ☐ Your lip drippeth over.
- ☐ I'll be double-damned!
- ☐ I was set up like two chicks in a beer commercial. They get into a fight and then they kiss and make up.
- ☐ My life is complete
- ☐ I wrote her a letter but I couldn't spell "yuck"—and that's all I had to say.
- ☐ It's all being done with Pop-Tarts and magic mirrors.
- ☐ If I ever get a gold medal, I'll have it bronzed.
- ☐ Do us a favor and quit acting your shoe size.
- ☐ Ahoy!
- ☐ Chuck Norris does not sleep. He waits.
- ☐ Don't get your nuts in a twist.
- ☐ My work is fallible but usually well-researched.
- ☐ Mayday! Mayday!
- ☐ I would rather have hot lead poured in my ears.
- ☐ As American as Apple computers.
- ☐ My wife can read me like the Sunday paper.
- ☐ I'm just a dedicated laborer in corporate America's vineyard.
- ☐ If neediness and desperation made for good looks, I'd look great.
- ☐ It is almost sinful to take money from the Federal government.
- ☐ I think we have some unfinished business.
- ☐ I plead contemporary insanity.
- ☐ Sorry, cuz!
- ☐ God bless you and everyone connected to you.

- ☐ My friends call me "Bleeding Gums."
- ☐ George Bush hates stem cells...but what he really hates is stem cell phones.
- ☐ My baby does the Hanky-Panky.
- ☐ You have your crazy corroded tongue in my girlfriend's mouth.
- ☐ This is no penny-ante game
- ☐ Good morning, Cleveland!
- ☐ This time, we're really going to get that McHale!
- ☐ I'll kiss a fat lady's ass!
- ☐ Don't try to lay no boogie-woogie on the king of rock and roll!
- ☐ I only give negative feedback.
- ☐ I'm a procrastinator...but I'll tell you about that sometime later.
- ☐ Never use your home as an ATM to pay for your kid's college.
- ☐ I like my women like I like my coffee, in a Styrofoam cup.
- ☐ I was born very young.
- ☐ Allow me to introduce myselves.
- ☐ You've been nothing but help.
- ☐ I wouldn't piss on you if you were on fire.
- ☐ He puts the "cooter" in "scooter."
- ☐ The search for excellence goes south.
- ☐ Take the steam out of you.
- ☐ I had a hat like that before my mom got a job.
- ☐ Check, please!
- ☐ This carpet needs a haircut.
- ☐ I grew up in a Norman Rockwell painting.
- ☐ This ain't the big rock candy mountain.
- ☐ I've been to some rodeos.
- ☐ My ass is grass!
- ☐ I'm not playing Lawrence Welk music here.

- ☐ Pipe down!
- ☐ I've got a hankerin' to go out west.
- ☐ My other car is a piece of shit, too.
- ☐ Now this dates me...
- ☐ I've done back flips for him.
- ☐ I'd sell mud if I knew how to make it.
- ☐ You are correct, sir!
- ☐ Get the ship into the channel
- ☐ This seems to be a new and unleashed side of you.
- ☐ I'm a byproduct of artificial intelligence.
- ☐ How canny of you to notice.
- ☐ I'm not a doctor but I'd be happy to take a look.
- ☐ Hey look, an iridium flux capacitor.
- ☐ I'm not wearing any hemp!
- ☐ My name is Ginger, Ginger Snap.
- ☐ I made it clear to my children early on, don't ever touch me.
- ☐ "Oh, bother," said Pooh as he couldn't find the pin to the grenade.
- ☐ There is no 1-800 number for that situation.
- ☐ Let my people go!
- ☐ I hope your sink stops up!
- ☐ That experience rearranged my DNA.
- ☐ The only thing pumping through my veins is a healthy respect for the badge.
- ☐ Don't do me any favors.
- ☐ I don't play Dixieland, but I do play border states.
- ☐ You don't care a hill of beans about me.
- ☐ Listen, Bub...
- ☐ That resonates with me.
- ☐ Game on!
- ☐ Eric will take your lunch money.
- ☐ I'm as happy as a schoolboy!

- [ ] Like heck I will!
- [ ] What the dickens?
- [ ] Now we're hauling meat!
- [ ] Six ways to Christmas!
- [ ] You're still out.
- [ ] We have both kinds of dancing here: square and clutch-and-hug.
- [ ] I'm allergic to negative feedback.
- [ ] Not cricket
- [ ] You reptile!
- [ ] That party was a real drinkeroo.
- [ ] Hakuna matata!
- [ ] And in conclusion: I'm finished speaking.

12. Now That's Funny

If anybody could make you squirt milk out your nose, it would be Uncle Boogs. Like the one time I went to the nursing home to have breakfast with him. As I joined him at the table, the server asked, "What will you have, honey?" "The same as him: Raisin Bran, extra milk." I replied. Well before you know it, both of us were laughing and giggling and snorting and making such a mess. I'm not sure, but I think a raisin popped out of Uncle Boogs's nose.

- ☐ Carl offered to help me move and bring packing boxes from work…Pizza Hut.
- ☐ "My dad taught me to swim by tying my hands and legs together, rowing me to the middle of the lake and throwing me in."
  "Ernie, he wasn't trying to teach you to swim."
- ☐ I almost got in a fight, but then I pulled out my "No-Hassle" card and they went away.
- ☐ You can't second guess your wife, but you can second guess your boss.
- ☐ Electric blanket super-setting—"Fish and Bacon."
- ☐ The reason Mayberry was so peaceful and quiet was because nobody was married. Andy, Aunt Bea, Barney, Floyd, Howard, Goober, Gomer, Earnest T. Bass, Helen, Thelma Lou, Clara, and, of course, Opie were all single. The only married person was Otis. Need I say more?
- ☐ The world's oldest typewriter types in pencil.
- ☐ My life is graded as a C+. May not get me into heaven, but perhaps a celestial vocational school.

- ☐ People are always confusing Carol Bunker with Archie O'Conner.
- ☐ Mom died, age 83 after a long battle with…a bear. She was a fighter.
- ☐ Track event: the low jump—You stand on a chair and see how far you can jump.
- ☐ You know that it was a good night at the bar when just before you fall asleep at 2:00 a.m., the toilet seat hits you on the head.
- ☐ You know you're in trouble when Tom Bodett picks you up at the airport.
- ☐ I don't mind tempting fate. But I don't want to give it a lap dance.
- ☐ What's wrinkled and hangs out your underwear? Mom.
- ☐ I don't want to bring a box cutter to a knife fight.
- ☐ I guess I just prefer to see the dark side of things. The glass is always half-empty. And cracked. And I just cut my lip on it. And I chipped a tooth…
- ☐ I recently went to a new doctor and noticed he was located in something called the Professional Building. I felt better right away.
- ☐ Dustbuster Olympics, Bronze, thank you very much.
- ☐ Knock knock—Interrupting Cow.
- ☐ The cult of cheerfulness.
- ☐ All purpose, self-rising dog.
- ☐ Permit me to introduce you to my oversexed spouse.
- ☐ Nobody knows how dry I am, but nobody seems to give a damn.
- ☐ The woman who returned her computer complaining that the foot pedal didn't work.
- ☐ Canned-ham humor.
- ☐ As a kid, we were allowed one new crayon a day, and we looked forward to it.
- ☐ Charles Dickens orders a martini, and the bartender says "…an olive or twist?"

- ☐ She was wearing a Mount Rushmore T-shirt and Lincoln and Washington were particularly prominently displayed.
- ☐ Every time I visit a Hobby Lobby, somebody cuts a corner off my man card.
- ☐ So, the trooper asks if I have a form of identification other than a fishing license...
- ☐ The Energizer Bunny was arrested and charged with battery.
- ☐ Demosthenes practiced speaking with a mouth of stones.
- ☐ I like cats, too. Let's exchange recipes!
- ☐ That's actually a two-part question and I can't answer either part.
- ☐ In grad school, I always tried to color between the lines.
- ☐ ...and then I realized the doc was actually a ventriloquist and it was his DUMMY who was giving the exam.
- ☐ Tombstone..."I knew this was going to happen!"
- ☐ The bagels of war were sounded.
- ☐ The moon was yellow and I was pretty chicken, too.
- ☐ A nuclear-powered ice cream machine—no meltdowns.
- ☐ We call it Thanksgiving Day but the turkeys call it Murder Day.
- ☐ The nutjob carpool...it met at work.
- ☐ I didn't know we had an awareness action plan.
- ☐ Did you hear about the dyslexic guy who walked into a bra?
- ☐ "What's this fly doing in my soup?" "The back stroke."
- ☐ Can't swing a dead cat without hitting someone with peanut allergies.
- ☐ Pre-traumatic Stress Syndrome.
- ☐ Don't be a douche—pardon my French, but douche IS French.
- ☐ Baby diary: "Day one, still tired from the move."
- ☐ I found a ruler in my son's bathroom.

- People say I have the body of Michael Phelps. If he knew what I was doing with it, he'd be mad as hell.
- Where did I go on my senior trip? Vietnam.
- Just once I'd like to be passed on the highway and not have people point at one of my tires.
- She wore a remote-control bra.
- When the going gets tough, the tough use duct tape.
- Didn't have money for cab fare, so I ordered a pizza to be delivered, then asked if I could ride along
- Just call me. You know how to dial me—put your finger in the hole and spin it.
- Whenever I try to balance my checkbook, the computer banks in NASA start kicking on and satellite dishes start re-aligning themselves.
- It seemed like it was about four years ago…no, wait, that was yesterday.
- Most engineers think they know everything. And they usually do.
- I changed my iPod's name to *Titanic.* It's syncing now.
- I feel like I'm living in television land.
- There will be a paperless workplace when there's a paperless bathroom.
- Don't beat a dead horse in the mouth.
- There is no divorce in Italy and only Catholics can get it.
- "He really takes the cake." "Where does he take the cake? Why not a pie?"
- The movie *The Birds?* I thought it was a documentary.
- They laughed at Joan of Arc, but she went right ahead and built it anyway.
- We could kiss better if we didn't have noses.
- Stress is when you wake up screaming and you realize you aren't asleep yet.
- Golf…you've got to visualize your shot before you hit it—that's why I start swearing in the backswing.

☐ "Hey watch this…" an idiot's last words.

☐ I remember when Aunt Joan and I were alone together in the kitchen during Thanksgiving. She's wearing red lipstick, and a tight sweater and she says to me, "Go ahead, you can touch 'em." Turns out, she was talking about the cranberries.

☐ Her mouth is so full of kisses, I can't get a word on edgewise.

☐ School fight song: *Dueling Banjos*

☐ Your mother must have had it tough, not having any children.

☐ I'm NOT sugar coating it. I'm lying.

☐ Cancer talk…"I lost a testicle. Not to cancer, to the insurance company."

☐ Upside down and backwards.

☐ My spouse and I only have sex once a week. Hopefully it's the same night.

☐ He has a case of leprosy, so don't shake his hand too hard.

☐ This girl today said she recognized me from the Vegetarians Club, but I'd swear I've never met herbivore.

☐ The location of your mailbox shows you how far away from your house you can roam in a robe before you start looking like a mental patient.

☐ Dancing cheek to cheek (tired of sitting on a chair after an hour)

☐ Speed reading accident—he hit a bookmark

☐ You'd have a better chance of finding a three-legged ballerina.

☐ Mail your packages early so the post office can lose them in time for Christmas.

☐ I still keep a picture of you in my locket. Naturally I had to cut off your hair to make it fit.

☐ If life was fair, Elvis would be alive and all the impersonators would be dead.

- ☐ I want to die peacefully in my sleep like my grandfather, rather than terrified and screaming like his passengers.
- ☐ Teach driver's ed and sex ed in the same car.
- ☐ Whenever we have roast beef, my wife puts two in the oven, one larger than the other. When the small one burns the other is ready.
- ☐ For three days after death, hair and fingernails continue to grow but phone calls taper off.
- ☐ I fell down the steps for 25 minutes while on the escalator.
- ☐ The difference between a Hoover vacuum cleaner and a Harley? The position of the dirt bag.
- ☐ What do you call a nun who sleep walks? A roamin' Catholic.
- ☐ A sign that you're getting old: a picture of you at a mortuary titled "coming soon."
- ☐ I heard you twice the first time.
- ☐ My kitchen qualified as a superfund site.
- ☐ Warning: Objects in mirror are dumber than they appear.
- ☐ We have only one person to blame, and that's each other.
- ☐ Priests get ADD—Advent Distress Disorder
- ☐ Get your tongue out of my mouth 'cause I'm kissing you goodbye.
- ☐ My sixty-year kindergarten reunion is coming up soon and I'm worried about the 125 pounds I've gained since then.
- ☐ BBQ...some people's religious experience
- ☐ I was so happy, I didn't know whether to spit or go blind.
- ☐ No matter how much you push the envelope, it'll still be stationery.
- ☐ You think you're better than I am just because you have two nuts.
- ☐ I know a guy who's addicted to drinking brake fluid, but he says he can stop any time.
- ☐ The meanest thing you can say to a woman without cursing: "You look fat when you cry."

- ☐ Ready, fire, aim!
- ☐ The Israel dairy farm: Cheeses of Nazareth
- ☐ Why is a banjo like a lawyer? People like them best when the case is closed.
- ☐ The fat lady sank.
- ☐ Lighting struck him in the head, melted his fillings, and soldered his jaw shut.
- ☐ My job at Sunday school was trying to keep the little people from sticking pins in their eyes.
- ☐ You hear about the masochist who likes a cold shower in the morning, so he takes a hot one?
- ☐ Bare-footed fetus
- ☐ You know your hotel is bad when your room isn't ready because forensics isn't done with it yet.
- ☐ My wife thinks the Olympics it too competitive.
- ☐ So I says to the waitress, "Do you have frog legs? If so hop back to the kitchen and get me some soup."
- ☐ His desk was a table from the Kobe Steak house.
- ☐ Phi Beta Ditto
- ☐ I just submitted my application to the Optimists Club…but I don't think they'll take me.
- ☐ He who laughs last didn't get the joke.
- ☐ When Bill sings, it makes your hair hurt and garage doors as far away as Dayton open.
- ☐ When I win the lottery, I'll have a basket of puppies delivered to my house every morning. I need something to feed my condor!
- ☐ Long ago, when I was just a fetus…
- ☐ Cockles of your heart? Technically, they're ventricles.
- ☐ Nothing to eat but stale cheese…
- ☐ If you're calling from a rotary dial phone, I'm sorry. Hang up and call from a touch tone phone. Welcome to the 80's.
- ☐ I'm waiting for caller IQ.
- ☐ All seriousness aside…

- ☐ A dentist and a manicurist married. They fought tooth and nail.
- ☐ The automated factory of the future will only contain two employees, a man and a dog. The man will be there to feed the dog, and the dog will be there to keep the man from touching the equipment.
- ☐ If God didn't want men to hunt, he wouldn't have given them plaid shirts.
- ☐ My therapist says I have a preoccupation with vengeance. We'll see about that.
- ☐ Jesus of Nazareth? I'm Dave of St. Louis.
- ☐ A phone is a seldom used app on my phone and I get mad when I'm forced to use it.
- ☐ Danger could be my middle name, but it's actually Warren.
- ☐ A recent study has found that women who carry a little extra weight live longer than the men who mention it.
- ☐ The peaceful atom
- ☐ My wife and I play an old game: "Does this belong here?"
- ☐ When I was your age, I only got an orange for Christmas and was damned happy to get it.
- ☐ New Year's resolution: Don't eat boogers.
- ☐ Cream of the crop
- ☐ Deja-pay-per-vu: thinking you've seen a movie on cable before.
- ☐ Those jokes are nursing home material.
- ☐ Puget Sound Effects Society
- ☐ You've made some extraordinary claims, and at the risk of sounding realistic...
- ☐ I tried to log in on my iPad. Turns out it was an Etch-a-Sketch and I don't own an iPad. Also, I'm out of vodka.
- ☐ A Geiger counter is useful in finding Marie Curie's gravesite.
- ☐ My favorite sport: cigar smoking, singles or mixed doubles

- ☐ Business class, economy coach, and jammy pants class
- ☐ Break these big concepts into smaller, more easily digestible chunks of knowledge.
- ☐ If I had a dollar for every girl that found me unattractive, they would eventually find me attractive.
- ☐ While I was walking in the woods, a tree fell and I didn't hear it.
- ☐ There comes a time in your life when you realize you'll never kiss Jennifer Aniston or Loni Anderson or Gillian Anderson. But I draw the line at Gilligan.
- ☐ I have ex-wives that haven't even been born yet.
- ☐ I worked so hard today…after I got home and ate dinner, about an hour later a knock at the door…it was my ass just now getting home.
- ☐ Paid $2,000 worth of engine work on a rental car
- ☐ I clapped because it's finished, not because I like it.
- ☐ I usually only slow dance with strangers at bars after a few beers.
- ☐ Not really a Starbucks, they just proudly serve Starbucks
- ☐ There once was a man named McClintercourse…
- ☐ I'm having a salmon day. That's when you swim upstream all day and get screwed in the end.
- ☐ It was nice cheating with you.
- ☐ I bit my tongue, not on purpose.
- ☐ I avoided her like I avoid the guy with a clipboard outside Trader Joe's.
- ☐ Bedford Falls revisited
- ☐ No smoking in my car with a baby aboard, unless you crack a window.
- ☐ George Washington's brother Carl was the Uncle of our Country.
- ☐ A duck goes into a bar, orders a beer. The Bartender says, "We don't serve ducks here."
  The duck replied, "With these prices I'm not surprised."

- ☐ You need to take a big drink of shut-up juice!
- ☐ You don't talk to the monkey when you can talk to the organ grinder.
- ☐ I don't know what's bothering you, but I bet it's hard to pronounce.
- ☐ Gamma Fields, a new subdivision
- ☐ Press 4 to hear an uplifting message about how we're not going to be bought out.
- ☐ I got a call from the police department saying they wanted to interview me. But I can't remember what job I applied for.
- ☐ Not my cup of meat
- ☐ They determined the speed of light by shining it through molasses and slowing it down.
- ☐ Wal-Mart, a mom-and-pop shop that got their shit together
- ☐ Want to keep guns out of schools? Stamp on them: "These guns were made with machines that may have been used to process tree nuts."
- ☐ In high school orchestra, she played third fiddle.
- ☐ If I wanted some smoke blown up my ass, I'd stay at home with a pack of Kools and a piece of rubber tubing.
- ☐ So-and-so will be eating Brazil nuts on location.
- ☐ The judge ordered that the horse thief be publicly strangled, not hanged.
- ☐ When you get a bladder infection, urine trouble.
- ☐ There are three rules for creating humor, but unfortunately, nobody knows what they are.
- ☐ Robbing Peter to pay the piper
- ☐ Vegetarian Moving Company: "We don't move anything over 15 pounds."
- ☐ He was an enigma wrapped in bacon, inside a crescent roll.
- ☐ How many men does it take to change a roll of toilet paper? Only one, but it has never happened yet.

- Heard of a nuclear family? Mine's a nuclear reactor.
- Why do men die before their wives? Because they want to.
- When you cross a pit bull with a collie, you get a dog that will chew off your leg and run for help.
- Monty Hall stumped the whole audience when he offered $50 for any shred of decency and self-respect.
- Burning the midnight oil at both ends
- Country song: *Who Poured Lye on My Dog?*
- I heard that some of the smart bombs are refusing to drop.
- That feeling we get in the cockles of our heart. Perhaps below our cockles, perhaps the sub-cockle region. Maybe in the kidney, maybe in the liver, maybe even in the colon.
- Can I interest you in a nightcap? No thanks, I don't wear one.
- Not "in the cloud"…the nuclear power industry calls it "in the plume."
- Grandmother wanted to be buried in Cook County, so she could vote after she's dead.
- Tombstone…"I told you I was sick!"
- If you want the truth, ask me. If you want something sugar-coated, go eat a doughnut.
- Trying to thread a needle with a haystack
- Answering machine…"Am I on the air?"
- Give me a fresh day, golf clubs, and a good partner…and forget about the golf.
- Signs all over the casino: Call 1-800-BETS-OFF if you have a gambling question. So I asked, "I've got a 10 and a 4. Should I stick or hit?"
- What do you do with an elephant with three balls? Walk him and pitch to the rhino.
- My favorite cassette tape: "Head Cleaner"
- No longer accepting compliments

- ☐ "I was shot in the leg during the war."
  "Do you have a scar?"
  "No, I don't smoke."
- ☐ "Anal-cranial inversion"—I think I know what that really means.
- ☐ I have amnesia and deja vu at the same time.
- ☐ The merge lane a.k.a. the "stop and cause a pile-up" and "jump out in front of somebody" lane.
- ☐ The Kardashian clan was so big that when they came down with flu, the doctor sent them to Bed, Bath & Beyond.
- ☐ It's not exactly rocket surgery.
- ☐ You know you're a stoner if you have a different color headband for every day of the week.
- ☐ "I'll bet you a dollar to a doughnut." That was back when doughnuts were ten cents.
- ☐ "Next Rest Area 25 miles"…that's a big rest area.
- ☐ Haunted French pancakes give me the crepes.
- ☐ As the band played *The Last Cheater's Dance*…
- ☐ Me: "That's an entirely different plan altogether." Everybody all together: "That's an entirely different plan."
- ☐ You don't bring a date to a wedding. That's like bringing a deer carcass to a hunting trip.
- ☐ England has no kidney bank, but it does have a Liverpool.
- ☐ At the bank I said, "I want to check my balance." So the teller pushed me out in front of traffic.
- ☐ A will is a dead giveaway.
- ☐ She could tell a dirty joke that would make you tinkle your pants.
- ☐ That college is advertised in *Hot Rod Magazine.*
- ☐ Bring the rental car back with a full tank. That's what the garden hose was there for.
- ☐ Honk if you love Jesus. If you want to meet him, text while driving.

- ☐ Happiness is being stuck in an elevator and discovering the ravishing blonde with you is a liquor salesperson with a case of samples.
- ☐ Country song: *I'm Down to My Last Broken Heart*
- ☐ Paranoia: An Art Form
- ☐ Tombstone: "What are you staring at?"
- ☐ "Meat Patty." That's how the butcher introduces his wife.
- ☐ I remember that I never got attention from girls till I got my braces off...my legs.
- ☐ He took me to a little out-of-the-way place that serves great Viking food.
- ☐ This is not goodbye...it is just that I won't see you again.
- ☐ Pass the biscuits, please,
- ☐ My favorite drink is Irish Coffee, because I like my coffee like I like my women: loaded with booze.
- ☐ Mr. Goodwrench goes to college.
- ☐ Writing things down is the best secret of a good memory.
- ☐ Peasant hunting...so mean.
- ☐ She's a whiskey maker's daughter but I love her still.
- ☐ Public toilets in Paris: Clean or free. Pick one.
- ☐ The police officer visited me and said my dogs were chasing people on bicycles. My dogs don't even know how to ride bicycles.
- ☐ What do you get when you roll a grenade onto the floor of a French restaurant? Linoleum Blonapart.
- ☐ Little Miss Muffet sat on a tuffet, eating her curds and whey. Along came a spider, who sat down beside her and said, "Hey, what's in the bowl, honey?"
- ☐ Country song: *If the Phone Didn't Ring it Was Me*
- ☐ On vacation, we stayed at the Henry Cabot Lodge.
- ☐ You say I'm a witch, like it's a bad thing.
- ☐ My parents remind me of *American Gothic.*
- ☐ Asked my dad if he would take me ice skating. He said, "Wait till it gets little warmer."

- ☐ A house with wall-to-wall floors.
- ☐ I called a neighbor and said that I was trying to take a nap, and could he turn down the stereo. I told him the door was open and to let himself in.
- ☐ Had a little trouble with constipation. The doctor prescribed some suppositories. For all the good they did, I could have stuck them up my ass!
- ☐ I'm not laughing at you. I'm laughing with the people who are laughing at you.
- ☐ This is the not the cholesterol-choked artery of yesterday.
- ☐ A microwave fireplace—you can lay down in front of a fire all night and it only takes eight minutes.
- ☐ I wear a patina of student loan debt.
- ☐ The worst time to have a heart attack is during game of charades.
- ☐ "It was 1992…not the year, my cholesterol."
- ☐ "You hang up." "No, you hang up."
- ☐ "Nuclear science is the zenith of atomic science and is essential for the further if civilization…"
  —Chernobyl dedication speech (Seriously!)
- ☐ And for the vegetarians, two unpeeled carrots.
- ☐ A large-bellied, middle-aged woman in a shapeless housedress answered the door. The nine-year-old Cub Scout asked, "Would you like to buy some popcorn?"
- ☐ She doesn't even take the cigarette out of her mouth before she tells the state trooper "kiss my ass."
- ☐ Today a man knocked on my door and asked for a small donation towards the local swimming pool. I gave him a glass of water.
- ☐ The flatted fifth, augmented fourth—the devil's chord.
- ☐ The first rule about Fight Club is not to talk about Fight Club. Unless you want to tell somebody about it.
- ☐ His cereal bowl comes with a lifeguard.
- ☐ They removed the pitcher from the game for throwing too hard.

☐ "Good" grief…as opposed to…?

☐ I'm losing my short-term memory, and also my short-term memory.

☐ I feel like I interrupted a pillow fight.

☐ Over the river and through the woods is how grandmother used to drive.

☐ I heard the nursing home welded a pair of ski boots to the bottom of the shower to prevent slipping.

☐ Silence of the Yams

☐ Paprika on potato salad is considered show-offish.

☐ After I die, I hope my wife doesn't sell my ukuleles, golf equipment, and fishing gear for what I told her I paid for it.

☐ Maybe not a full-blown heart attack, perhaps a semi attack. My heart wasn't REALY attacked, but I DID hear footsteps in the weeds. Maybe it was only a twig, or maybe my whole aorta was about to fall off.

☐ I bought a pack of batteries and they weren't included so I had to buy them again.

☐ Our Lady of Sorrows Urgent Care

☐ Danger: Spooky Stuff Inside

☐ The difference between a bellboy and a bellhop? The bellboy has two legs.

☐ If variety is the spice of life, marriage is the big can of leftover Spam.

☐ A black guy, a woman, and a Mormon walk into a bar…or run for president…It was 2008.

☐ Guy: "Have you ever been so drunk and lay down in bed and feel the room spin?"
Girl: "Yes."
Guy: "This is going to be my lucky night…"

☐ The first time I met Gene Rayburn, I said to him _____

☐ True romance is when the lovely couple shares one of those tiny pieces of trident gum.

☐ I met my wife in Vietnam, but she's from Ohio.

- ☐ If "if's" and "and's" were pots and pans, there'd be no need for tinkerers.
- ☐ Canes can be found in the cruise ship Lost & Found.
- ☐ I was so naive as a kid, I used to sneak behind the barn and do nothing.
- ☐ You can count those with the fingers on one hand and still be able to bowl.
- ☐ That third doughnut is the cause of my low-grade nausea.
- ☐ I keep a sawed off two-by-four in my car as a weapon.
- ☐ Eyebrows are sisters, not twins.
- ☐ You won't hear a single four-letter word from me. I don't go for that bullshit.
- ☐ Schadenfreude was the most popular cocktail served in that bar.
- ☐ When I was your age I was six.
- ☐ The way to exude confidence is to walk around with a smile like you know a sexy secret.
- ☐ Carl was holding a pound-and-a-half of Aunt Betty's nut butter.
- ☐ William the Bastard became William the Conqueror. (It's true!)
- ☐ My wife wanted to go someplace expensive for dinner. I took her to the airport and then to the stadium.
- ☐ If women didn't take so long to get ready, men would never check their car's oil.
- ☐ My parents never fought much. But they did have "evenings of candor."
- ☐ My Aunt Myrna shows up on the wedding reception dance floor, wearing a tight white dress, and through the fabric and her pantyhose you can see the outline of a tattoo on her fanny. You can't pick your family, right?
- ☐ Outback Steakhouse is for girlfriends. Fleming's is for your wife.

  Retired people don't go on vacations, they take trips. And book royalties help, thank you.

13. Questions

Typical dinner conversation with Uncle Boogs would go something like this, "If a doctor has a heart attack while performing surgery, will the other doctors and nurses present work on him first?"

Books and websites are loaded with these circular questions. There is no need to load this chapter with them. The questions found here are usually rhetorical, often insulting, and great conversation starters.

- ☐ Why don't you pull up a sofa and have a seat?
- ☐ Does your dog bite?
- ☐ The Hokey Pokey...would it be a shame if that's what it's *really* all about?
- ☐ Is nausea one of the twelve steps?
- ☐ Has the public consciousness become inert?
- ☐ And what lessons have you learned, Dorothy?
- ☐ If it smells like shit, but it has "Happy Birthday!" written on it with icing, what do YOU think it is?
- ☐ Have you ever noticed that anybody driving slower than you is an idiot, and anyone going faster than you is a maniac?
- ☐ What's wrong, Colonel Sanders? Chicken?
- ☐ Did you notice that there's a lot less oxygen in the room since she came in?
- ☐ What's the matter? Did a dog pee on your cinnamon toast?

- ☐ TWA finally returned my lost luggage. What will I do with bell bottoms?
- ☐ Do you kiss your mother with that dirty mouth?
- ☐ Was Humpty Dumpty wearing clean underwear?
- ☐ Are you smelling what I'm stepping in?
- ☐ What do you know? A sack of flour makes a big biscuit!
- ☐ Do I make myself conspicuous?
- ☐ Do you need a silencer when you shoot a mime?
- ☐ Did you hear about the crossed-eyed teacher who lost her job because she couldn't control her pupils?
- ☐ Will the circle be unbroken?
- ☐ Frontal lobotomy...What, there's another kind?
- ☐ How WAS you trained?
- ☐ Can Jerry's kids pay for stuff at 7-Eleven with money from the jar?
- ☐ Is your well deep enough?
- ☐ What is this, a handsome contest? (when among a lot of good-looking guys)
- ☐ Why do nomads squat?
- ☐ Were we separated at birth or what?
- ☐ If tin whistles are made of tin, what are fog horns made of?
- ☐ And which dwarf are you?
- ☐ You heard about the horse who got shot, then had to break her leg?
- ☐ Am I caller number seven?
- ☐ How many drams in a pennyweight?
- ☐ Why is it that babies need seat belts to eat?
- ☐ How are your elves?
- ☐ Four out of five people suffer from diarrhea. What's up with that other guy?
- ☐ Do you rhumba?
- ☐ What if you tied buttered toast to the back of a cat and dropped it?
- ☐ So, you have a better bad idea?

☐ How are you? Vigorous and potent!

☐ Would you like to join my club for mutual improvement?

☐ Who let him out of the dayroom?

☐ What kind of a Pee-Wee's Playhouse are you running?

☐ Is it time for your medication? Or mine?

☐ Kamikaze pilots...why the helmet?

☐ What am I, used Kleenex?

☐ Five Great Lakes...why is only one Superior?

☐ How am I? Bloated, constipated, got a boil on my ass the size of a walnut—you know, the usual.

☐ Are you picking up the wrath I'm putting down?

☐ Are you on drugs, or just stupid?

☐ Dig?

☐ My parents met in a bowling alley in the Bronx. You got a problem with that?

☐ Ever notice that when you drop a baby, it takes a few seconds for her to start crying?

☐ Just read that 4,153,237 people got married last year. Not to cause any trouble, but shouldn't that be an even number?

☐ Are you crackers?

☐ Are they rugged individuals or team players?

☐ What's new, pussycat?

☐ Are you allowed to leave the nursing home?

☐ What do you know? It takes a big hog to weigh a ton.

☐ An oxymoron? A moron who studies at Oxford?

☐ For identification, did Washington take out a quarter?

☐ Pardon me, am I protruding?

☐ Going down the tubes...what tube? How many tubes?

☐ "Can you put in a new engine?"
   "No, the old one is still in there."

☐ You old horndog, how's tricks?

☐ Where were you when the ship hit the sand?

☐ Where have you been, locked up in a biosphere?

☐ Why is my baby ugly?

☐ After a bad cup of coffee... "How could you eat something like that?"

☐ Who do you think I am, the Flying Nun?

☐ Remember when we used to have summer jobs?

☐ Why do they sing *Take Me Out to the Ball Game* when they're already there?

☐ "Are you all right?"
"All right? I think I'm perfect!"

☐ Who took the "fun" out of "dysfunctional?"

☐ Who do I look like, Nina Totenberg?

☐ Who are you going to call when something gets wrapped around the axle?

☐ How's my little hellcat?

☐ What do you do with a dead show girl?

☐ Does my personality invite ridicule?

☐ Country song: *How Long Does it Take a Memory to Drown?*

☐ Who would build on such quicksand?

☐ Why don't you ever get a busy signal on a wrong number?

☐ You remember Vietnam? It was in all the papers.

☐ Do I LOOK like a freakin' people person?

☐ Can you say that again? Without spitting?

☐ What size straight jacket should I order for you?

☐ Hey, what about Dorothy?

☐ How would you like a mouthful of teeth?

☐ Why do tug boats push barges?

☐ Does oatmeal have lumps?

☐ "You senile?"
"No. I haven't even been to Egypt."

☐ Where are we going and why am I in this hand basket?

☐ Does the plan have any firewalls?

☐ Why are you in such a good mood? Did you run over a squirrel?

☐ What are you doing in these waters?

☐ Are these your eyeballs? I found them in my cleavage.

☐ "O death, where is thy sting?"
   "The sting of death is sin."

☐ Was that Bill wearing a hat made of aluminum foil?

☐ I'm going to the bathroom. Do you want me to bring anything back for you?

☐ Do you know those life forms?

☐ "I'd be more than happy to."
   "How can you be more than happy?"

☐ Who do you think I am, Joe Mannix?

☐ Nice perfume. Must you marinate in it?

☐ Isn't that one of the signs of the apocalypse?

☐ Do you think I can conjure miracles?

☐ Did you hear about the guy who fell onto an upholstery machine last week? He's now fully recovered.

☐ Have you ever seen a talking emu? If you have, be careful, they're liars.

☐ How can camp latrines be so nasty when nobody has the courage to use them?

☐ Have you not noticed how my coat is so shiny?

☐ Any bats in the cave?

☐ "Why does it take four women to change a light bulb?"
   "IT JUST DOES."

☐ Smoking a little something from the Bobo tree, are we?

☐ Do you know any SHORT stories?

☐ Are you married or happy?

☐ Are you deciding on a snack or defrosting the refrigerator?

☐ "Did you just say something dirty?"
   "No."
   "Oh, would you?"

☐ Does anal-retentive have a hyphen?

- ☐ "What do you do for a living?"
  "Breathe."
- ☐ How in the blazes?
- ☐ How do I set a laser printer to stun?
- ☐ Who do you think I am, the Amazing Kreskin?
- ☐ Questions, comments, statements of fact, or fiction?
- ☐ Isn't she a dear?
- ☐ Have you ever imagined the world without hypothetical questions?
- ☐ Why don't you leave everything in my hands and I'll get in touch with you?
- ☐ What are you dribbling about?
- ☐ Could someone shed some light on this very dark room?
- ☐ What does that have to do with the price of cabbage?
- ☐ Can we fix it or do we need to hire a brain surgeon?
- ☐ And your cry-baby, whiney opinion would be...?
- ☐ Nice suit. Did you get any 8-tracks with it?
- ☐ "You want your milk in a bag?"
  "No, leave it in the bottle."
- ☐ Which twin has the Tony?
- ☐ What's keeping Jesus?
- ☐ Hello, this is the incontinence hotline, can you hold please?
- ☐ Did you complete the pre-mission matrix?
- ☐ How do I get in bed with...?
- ☐ What's the difference between a cuttlefish and a squid?
- ☐ Can you have a headache when you're sleeping?
- ☐ Why do people choose to video a delivery and not the conception?
- ☐ What was I saying before I chased that rabbit?
- ☐ Is the quantum leap a track event?
- ☐ Cold turkey vs. warm turkey
- ☐ Have you ever been "catfished" on a dating site?

14. People, Famous or Otherwise

Sometimes, Uncle Boogs would use people's names to make fun of you. He would combine the names in this chapter with good-natured ribbing. Like "Nice report, NINA TOTENBERG," "Hey EINSTEIN, zip your zipper," or "Nice catch, DIMAGGIO." Other people included in this chapter are nostalgic figures from the past.

- ☐ The Great Karnack
- ☐ The Wizard of Menlo Park
- ☐ Camptown ladies
- ☐ The Grand Inquisitor
- ☐ The unwashed masses
- ☐ Dr. Kevorkian
- ☐ Agnes Moorehead
- ☐ Saint Lethargious, patron saint of lethargy and procrastination
- ☐ United States Police Department
- ☐ Bobby McGee
- ☐ Spaz
- ☐ The Overlord
- ☐ Captain Acid
- ☐ The marginal and infirmed
- ☐ Monty Kempa
- ☐ Dough-eyed progressives
- ☐ Tom Foolery
- ☐ Sister Morphine

IN THIS DAY AND AGE, WORTHY MENTORS ARE HARD TO FIND. USE THESE CHECKBOXES TO IDENTIFY PEOPLE YOU MAY WANT TO LEARN MORE ABOUT.

- ☐ Aging Bohemians
- ☐ Booger-munchers
- ☐ Our Lady of the Worthless Miracle
- ☐ An old farmer grizzled in denim coveralls
- ☐ Samuel Homonym
- ☐ Morgan Fairchild
- ☐ Sebastian Cabot
- ☐ Olga, the mistress of death and the whore of Babylon
- ☐ Chef Boyardee
- ☐ Crazy Guggenheim
- ☐ The George Bush Dirty Tricks Committee
- ☐ Mack the knife
- ☐ Toots Nutzio
- ☐ Norman Rockwell
- ☐ The Radio Messiah
- ☐ Two-Buck Chuck
- ☐ Professor of Peace
- ☐ Pencil-necked geek
- ☐ The Lemon Pipers
- ☐ Cross-eyed stepchild
- ☐ Pippi Longstockings
- ☐ Sheriff Meatballs
- ☐ Panama Red
- ☐ Fat Tony
- ☐ Thick-headed commentators
- ☐ We are the potato people
- ☐ Zombies
- ☐ Vagrants and prostitutes
- ☐ Prince of Pizza
- ☐ The polka band Otto and the Schwein Puppies
- ☐ Sister Diesel Locomotive
- ☐ Willie Loman
- ☐ Skinny Ray

- ☐ The worthy poor
- ☐ The Truth Squad
- ☐ Crouching Dave
- ☐ Mr. Whipple
- ☐ Mr. French
- ☐ The Singing Nun
- ☐ Chess King
- ☐ Choo Choo Mama
- ☐ Sweetheart of Sigma Chi
- ☐ Holden Caulfield
- ☐ Lounge lizards
- ☐ Wally Ballou
- ☐ Charlie's Angels
- ☐ Barry Goldwater...the urologist
- ☐ The villagers
- ☐ Mr. Cold Shower
- ☐ Our Lady of Perpetual Responsibility
- ☐ The Pencil Pushing Department
- ☐ Gawky towheads
- ☐ Father McKenzie
- ☐ Brass hats
- ☐ The old gang at Yale
- ☐ Dim-minded peaceniks
- ☐ Nipsey Russell
- ☐ Poor bastard
- ☐ Judge Wapner
- ☐ Number Two Banana
- ☐ Worker bees
- ☐ Doodle Town Pipers
- ☐ Stumblebums
- ☐ Spritle and Chim Chim
- ☐ Dr. Democracy
- ☐ Aunt Sally

- ☐ Jack Ruby
- ☐ Mrs. Beasley
- ☐ Trust fund baby
- ☐ Spooky Alice
- ☐ Chumley and Tennessee Tuxedo
- ☐ Earnest Borgnine
- ☐ Our favorite goat toucher, Osama Bin Laden
- ☐ Nick "The Weasel" Testorinie
- ☐ Emmet Kelly
- ☐ Sister Holy Water
- ☐ Consortium of Concerned Trainers
- ☐ Count Chocula
- ☐ Jim Nabors
- ☐ Lug-headed kids
- ☐ The Potent One
- ☐ Digital natives
- ☐ Goldie Hawn
- ☐ They who walk among the golden candle sticks
- ☐ Citizen of the World
- ☐ The Seldom Home Boys
- ☐ Mr. Tambourine Man
- ☐ Mrs. Charming
- ☐ Maniacs and hard-drinking merchant seamen
- ☐ Neutron Jack
- ☐ Christina Statutory
- ☐ Malibu Barbie
- ☐ Don Rickles look-alikes
- ☐ Woodmen of the World (look it up!)
- ☐ St. Simeon, the Holy Fool
- ☐ Mr. Know-it-all
- ☐ Large Marge
- ☐ Swells and dandies
- ☐ Gloomy neurotics

- ☐ Mr. Wisenheimer
- ☐ Hunchback of Notre Dame
- ☐ The witch riding the vacuum cleaner
- ☐ Our forefathers and foremothers
- ☐ Varmints and ruffians
- ☐ Lilly Everwhite
- ☐ Buford Pusser
- ☐ Lieutenant Dan
- ☐ Aunt Blabby
- ☐ Snot-faced phlegm-wads
- ☐ Han Solo and Napoleon Solo, often confused
- ☐ Women of an accountable age
- ☐ Mr. Peabody and the Way-Back Machine
- ☐ Reefer Man
- ☐ Mr. Waverly
- ☐ Mungo Jerry
- ☐ Danny Yolksac
- ☐ Mother figure
- ☐ One of those people outside Trader Joe's with a clipboard
- ☐ Dr. Cocoa Puff
- ☐ Confidence man or confidence trickster (conman)
- ☐ Johnny Icepick
- ☐ Queen of Denial
- ☐ Sammy and the Fly Rod Boys
- ☐ Robert Goddard (a real rocket scientist)
- ☐ Twins born from different wombs
- ☐ The untutored
- ☐ Gaseous Clay
- ☐ The Gospel Humming Birds
- ☐ Atticus Finch
- ☐ French underground
- ☐ Skipper and Midge
- ☐ Al Einstein

- ☐ Sarcastic feminists
- ☐ Moon-faced liberals
- ☐ Dr. Pahpshmir
- ☐ Vladimir Tserijemiwtz
- ☐ Sandy Duncan Junior
- ☐ Bluegrass band: The Chip Kickers
- ☐ Peter Tork
- ☐ Our Lady of Relaxed Virtue
- ☐ Political, half-witted goobers wearing red MAGA hats
- ☐ Trainers for Social Responsibility
- ☐ Scooter Libby
- ☐ Larry Mondello
- ☐ Loggins and Messina
- ☐ Bowser from Sha Na Na
- ☐ Flip Wilson
- ☐ Jughead
- ☐ The Organization of Fisherman's Wives
- ☐ Zealot
- ☐ Bob Keeshan
- ☐ Miss Particle Board

15. Orphans Refusing to be Classified

By now you have observed that corralling these phrases into categories is not an exact science. Arguably, some are out of place. But as Uncle Boogs used to say, "Perfection is the enemy of completion." Or, "Done is better than good." Listed in this chapter are phrases and sayings who refused to be shoehorned into previous chapters.

- ☐ Circus of the Stars
- ☐ Note to self...
- ☐ Even-Steven
- ☐ You're foaming at the mouth.
- ☐ Cherokee Nation
- ☐ My peeps
- ☐ How canny of you to notice!
- ☐ With consequences for all
- ☐ You just made it move a little.
- ☐ Hardwiring
- ☐ The power to save the world
- ☐ More discoverable
- ☐ Surfaceblow and Associates
- ☐ When the ship hits the sand
- ☐ You underrate yourself.
- ☐ Turgid, verbose, shapeless, but pregnant with its message
- ☐ Congenitally adverse
- ☐ Wackadoo
- ☐ The guys in the engine room are guiding the ship.

- ☐ The President didn't have the power to muzzle the press.
- ☐ The trail of clues led me to your door.
- ☐ The George Bush Dirty Tricks Committee
- ☐ The point of failure
- ☐ Hunky Dory
- ☐ Even cowgirls get the blues.
- ☐ Here's your hat, what's your hurry?
- ☐ Over the moon
- ☐ The trip to Abilene
- ☐ On the other hand...
- ☐ Restaurants where the menus are coated in plastic and a family member is chained to the cash register
- ☐ It is my art form.
- ☐ I'm in the final minutes of the last day of my life.
- ☐ Degrees of bad
- ☐ I'll say it again for you.
- ☐ Steve proved more correct.
- ☐ For the good of the cause
- ☐ I watched his face turn to wood.
- ☐ Tone deaf
- ☐ For the purpose of domestic prosperity
- ☐ Good to see you've kept your sense of humor.
- ☐ One less egg to fry
- ☐ Thunderstruck
- ☐ Mind-numbing
- ☐ The choreography of getting to...
- ☐ Close to the bone
- ☐ You must not be from these parts.
- ☐ Joined at the hip
- ☐ You bowled a lot of strikes, but you left one standing.
- ☐ I got that on the first bounce.
- ☐ Jesus of Nazareth? I'm Dave of St. Louis.

☐ Died of dropsy

☐ Looks like I'm bringing a drunk girl home tonight!

About the Author

Dave Kempa has no credentials which would otherwise make him an authority on this publication. Nor does he have achievements that build credibility and that would be of interest to the reader. He has won no prizes, nor teaches at any credible educational institution. He holds no honorary degrees. He has written no other books and doesn't have a website.

He was, however, born 118 miles from Florida, Missouri, Mark Twain's birthplace. Maybe that's interesting.